Step Parenting
and the Blended Family

Step Parenting
and the Blended Family

Recognizing the problems and
overcoming the obstacles

by

Scott Wooding

Fitzhenery & Whiteside

Fitzhenry and Whiteside Limited, 195 Allstate Parkway, Markham, Ontario L3R 4T8

In the United States: 311 Washington Street, Brighton, Massachusetts 02135

www.fitzhenry.ca • godwit@fitzhenry.ca

Fitzhenry & Whiteside acknowledges with thanks the Canada Council for the Arts, and the Ontario Arts
Council for their support of our publishing program. We acknowledge the financial support of the
Government of Canada through the Book Publishing Industry Development Program (BPIDP) for our
publishing activities.

ONTARIO ARTS COUNCIL
CONSEIL DES ARTS DE L'ONTARIO

Recycled
Supporting responsible use
of forest resources
FSC www.fsc.org Cert no. SW-COC-1271
© 1996 Forest Stewardship Council

100%

Library and Archives Canada Cataloguing in Publication
Wooding, Scott
Step parenting and the blended family : recognizing the problems and
overcoming the obstacles / Scott Wooding.
ISBN 978-1-55455-024-1
1. Stepparents—Family relationships. 2. Stepfamilies. 3. Parenting.
I. Title.
HQ759.92.W66 2008   646.7'8   C2008-900265-2

United States Cataloguing-in-Publication Data
Wooding, Scott.
Step parenting and the blended family :
recognizing the problems and overcoming the obstacles / Scott Wooding.
[256] p. : col. ill. ; cm.
Summary: a comprehensive road map to successfully integrate parents and children.
ISBN: 9781554550241 (pbk.)
1. Stepparents—Family relationships. 2. Stepfamilies. 3. Parenting. I. Title.
646.7/8 dc22 HQ759.92.W66 2008

Cover design by Michelle C. Williams
Cover image by Getty - PhotoAlto / Eric Audras
Interior design by Karen Petherick Thomas
Printed and bound in Canada

1 3 5 7 9 10 8 6 4 2

ENVIRONMENTAL BENEFITS STATEMENT

Fitzhenry & Whiteside saved the following
resources by printing the pages of this book on
chlorine free paper made with 100% post-consumer
waste.

TREES	WATER	ENERGY	SOLID WASTE	GREENHOUSE GASES
27	9,870	19	1,267	2,378
FULLY GROWN	GALLONS	MILLION BTUs	POUNDS	POUNDS

Calculations based on research by Environmental Defense and the Paper Task Force.
Manufactured at Friesens Corporation

Contents

Introduction

The challenges of marriage are often underestimated in the glow of love that surrounds courtship and the early marital years. The clearest indicator of how difficult marriage can be is the divorce statistics. Currently the figures show that in the U.S. that rate is 3.6 divorces per thousand people, which is the highest figure in the world. In Canada that figure stands at 2.6, and although that seems much better, it is still the world's third-highest rate of divorce. While this statistic is good for comparison of divorce rates, even more telling is the percentage of marriages that last thirty years or more. In Canada (2002 figures) 37.6% of all marriages did not survive to the 30-year mark. In the U.S. the figures are frightening. According to *Divorce* magazine, only 20% of all marriages will make it to 35 years. It seems obvious, then, that maintaining a marriage over a long period is much more difficult than most people realize when they first enter the matrimonial state.

Another underestimated challenge is that of raising children. While it is relatively easy in the infant stages (although often physically exhausting, for the mother in particular), by the time the kids reach the teenage years, the majority of parents are gritting their teeth and hoping this phase will soon end. The statistics on teenage violence, drug use, smoking, and depression, outlined in my previous book, *The Parenting Crisis*, have all been on the rise in recent years. These figures clearly indicate the difficulty of raising a child in today's complex and fast-paced world. Unfortunately, most parents do not realize how demanding child-raising can be when they initially take on the task.

While marriage and child-raising are much more difficult than the majority of people who enter into these processes realize, they both pale in comparison to the challenge of stepparenting and blending families. It would seem logical that remarriages would be more stable than first marriages. After all, the brides and grooms are older and more experienced than they were for their first nuptials. Alas, remarriages have an even greater chance of dissolution than do the initial efforts. Dr. Samuel Johnson, the eighteenth-century writer, once said that second marriages were "the triumph of hope over experience," and this appears to be the case. In the U.S., 37% of second marriages end before they reach the 10-year anniversary, while in Canada 20% of second marriages end before the 8-year mark.

The possible reasons for this dismal second-marriage failure rate are outlined in a Statistics Canada paper published in 2006. These include:

- a personal psychology that makes a person unable to maintain relationships
- learned behaviour—people have solved their first marriage's problems by ending the relationship, so they follow this pattern
- lack of social support for remarriages, presumably from friends and relatives, and
- a smaller pool of available candidates for remarriage (all the good ones are taken), which reduces the chances of finding a suitable partner.

Unfortunately, for some reason, the paper's writers missed what is in this author's experience the most serious barrier to a successful remarriage. The great majority of today's remarriages involve unions where at

SCOTT WOODING

least one of the partners has children from the previous relationship. Most often it is the female who brings children into the relationship because women generally tend to get custody more often. However, this is not always the case, and, in fact, it is not unknown for both participants in the new marriage to bring their children to the marriage. As a result, either one or both of the parents becomes a stepparent. It is the stepparenting process that causes the greatest friction in second marriages, often for reasons only peripherally related to the nature of the children. Rare is the remarriage that recognizes the difficulties inherent in stepparenting and takes steps to counter these potential difficulties. That lack of foresight is clearly because so few people realize how difficult this process can be. To illustrate, here is a case history that points out two of the major causes of remarriage failure:

> *The first appointment with the mother, Julie, came in 1999. She brought her 10-year-old son, Dan, with her as she was worried about his moodiness and temper. Julie had recently remarried and was sharing custody of Dan and a younger girl with her ex-husband. At this time the problem appeared to be with the ex-husband, who was pushing Dan to excel in hockey, and thus frustrating the lad, as his skills were just average. No matter how she tried, Julie could not get her ex to see the damage he was doing to Dan. In fact, the harder she tried the more obstinate her ex became. Dan did appear to like his new stepfather Dave, who had two children of about the same ages, but was not particularly close to him at this point.*
>
> *After two appointments, where advice was given to Julie on how best to deal with her ex, Julie did not make any new ones, so that all appeared to be well—until four years later. While Dan was no longer showing any signs of a temper, he was not trying in school or in hockey—clear signs of a low self-concept, which was most likely the*

result of failing to meet his father's unrealistic expecta-
tions. However, this time the main problem was with Julie's
daughter, Erica, who was 13 at this time. She was refusing
to visit her real father at all, indicating a deep-rooted anger
with him, and was writing dark poetry and showing other
signs of depression. Erica reported that she hated her dad
and, while Dave was okay as a stepfather, he did not treat
her the same as he treated his own daughter. Suggestions,
including changing schools and a session with Julie and
Dave about being more consistent in their parenting styles,
were given for dealing with the depression.

It was two more years before new difficulties
appeared. This time Dave called for an appointment for
himself and his daughter, Jessica. She was apparently
skipping school and was flouting the house rules. The
problem was clearly one of needing attention from her
father, and so suggestions were made accordingly.
However, in the course of the interview a bombshell was
dropped. Julie and Dave were still married but were now
living in separate residences. This way the friction that
had been present over the past seven years between the
children and the parents, who still maintained different
parenting styles, was minimized. Julie visited often but
everyone seemed happier, except possibly Jessica, who had
obviously formed a bond with Julie.

Of the four children involved in this blended family, three developed
emotional problems severe enough to require the intervention of a psychologist. Even worse, the marriage did not survive this turmoil. Two
causes can be pinpointed for the problems of the children and the collapse
of the marriage. The first was the inability of Julie and her ex-husband to
resolve the animosity between them, causing both her children to have
subsequent emotional difficulties. This is a huge problem for remarriages

SCOTT WOODING

and one of the main causes of their failure. The second was the inconsistent parenting styles of Dave and Julie which, despite several counselling sessions, were never properly resolved. In his final session with the therapist, Dave actually stated, "You can take more from your own than you can from the other kids." This should not be the case. Dave did not realize that a key factor in blending families is to treat all children as equally as possible, no matter who the biological parent is. Again, the inability of the parents to agree on a common parenting style created serious problems for the children and friction between the parents. The real tragedy in this case is that Julie and Dave still love each other but they just couldn't manage to blend their families effectively.

While blending families is clearly more difficult than simply adding a stepparent to an existing family, many common problems exist between these two situations. The most common one is the almost universal inability of grown people to move on from their first marriages. The bitterness and animosity that pervade the divorce process do not end with remarriage. Rather they tend to poison the new union, particularly when children are involved. They add stress to the life of one parent that makes the difficult process of stepparenting even harder. Added to this is the complexity of parenting children with whom you do not share a biological bond. Children tend to be much more forgiving of a biological parent due to the bond between them that has existed from birth. Stepparents get no such latitude so that the disagreements that occur, especially during the teen years, become more bitter with a stepparent than they would be with the natural one.

These are the major problems encountered in stepparenting and blending families and, along with others that are also covered in this book, are the major hurdles that stepparents must overcome in order to have a successful remarriage and to raise emotionally stable children. These are not difficult problems to solve if everyone involved is trying, but unfortunately this is rarely the case. The power of emotions over reason and logic is frightening, and since most couples plunge into remarriage without recognizing the huge hurdles involved in stepparenting and blending families, these emotions often tend to overwhelm reason and logic, and another marriage ends in dissolution.

Parenting also tends to be charged with emotion and many adults have difficulty taking parenting advice, either from their new spouse, who is often the biological parent of the children, or even from experts in the field. However, this advice can often be the key to the success of a remarriage, and it should be sought immediately once parenting differences surface.

These are the topics that this book will address. Unlike most books on this topic, it will not start with the new marriage but will instead begin with the breakup of the old one, since it is the baggage from the first marriage that so often interferes with the success of the next one. After the breakup is dissected, the book moves into the courtship period because, even before a new marriage occurs, the children of the previous one are involved. This is another area that most books do not deal with in detail, but which is also critical to the success of a remarriage.

Once the new marriage has occurred, there are a number of issues that are unique to it that likely were not problems in the first one. These issues are often ignored or not recognized in the glow of a new love, but they must be addressed if the marriage is to survive. This book tackles these issues from a practical rather than a theoretical standpoint, with the frequent use of case histories to illustrate the main points.

Finally, there are a number of related issues that stepparents often need help with. These include discipline methods, which even first marriages, struggle with in today's parenting climate, teenage issues, which are difficult even for biological parents, and grandparenting issues. The latter are consistently overlooked in remarriages but can be a huge concern for the kids and for the new stepparent. Because blended families have problems that are unique, a separate chapter is devoted to each of these issues.

The emphasis throughout this book will be on practical and useful advice delivered in an easily digested format. It will attempt to cover as many situations as possible, since there are many different combinations of second marriage partners, and will be illustrated with many examples

SCOTT WOODING

from the author's 35-year counselling history. It is this author's belief that, barring marriages where one of the partners has a serious mental illness or addiction, all remarriages involving children can be successful with the proper preparation and attitude.

Breakup Baggage

Marriages in most of the modern world usually happen as a result of the powerful feelings generated by love. These incredibly euphoric feelings cause lovers to want to spend their entire lives together and usually to have children. Research has shown that these feelings are caused by a cocktail of brain chemicals, including dopamine, endorphins, serotonin, oxytocin, and vasopressin. Released during the early phase of love, these chemicals result in such intense feelings of pleasure, excitement, and rapture that poets have waxed eloquent over them for hundreds of years. Suddenly the person in love can think of almost nothing but this potential mate and wants these feelings to last forever. Marriage often follows shortly thereafter.

Unfortunately, these intense feelings are apparently not biologically designed to last much past the short period of time required to procreate the species by having children. After this all-too-short period of time, the feelings moderate to a calmer form that tends to last longer. This phase is characterized by feelings of calmness, security, and social comfort. Nice feelings, but with none of the fireworks of what is often called the romantic or attraction phase. According to love theorists, it is during this time period that the parenting process is supposed to occur. Unfortunately, this conversion from intense romantic love to the more tranquil version often creates confusion among marital partners.

According to Dr. Helen Fisher of Rutgers University, the chemical attraction that we call love is at its most powerful in the early stages of a relationship, probably due to ancient biological needs to produce children and thus maintain the species. Dr. Fisher believes that love comes in three stages—lust, attraction, and attachment. Lust is the craving for sex that develops during puberty and that is necessary to begin the process of mating. This is often called "puppy love" and is very strong during the teenage years. This is followed by the attraction or romantic love phase, a refinement of the lust phase that makes it possible to select a mate. It is this stage that most people remember as "love" because the feelings are by far the most intense and pleasurable. The final or attachment phase is the time period during which children are raised. The feelings during this stage are those of calmness, security, social comfort, and emotional union. They do not resemble the romantic love feelings and are not nearly as exciting. _____

This confusion is the result of people feeling that their love has diminished or even died completely. They don't realize that this is just a natural stage in the biological progression of love. The end of this euphoric period of love also brings with it a clearer look at the qualities of the marital partner, qualities that were either ignored or not noticed in the early stages of the relationship. The old expression "love is blind" is often found to be a sad reality. Gradually spouses realize that those qualities they initially found charming, or dismissed as just occasional lapses, are actually permanent features of their loved one's personality. An example of this might be the realization that the intense interest that the spouse showed in the partner's activities in the early days, which seemed to indicate how much he or she cared, is actually controlling and manipulative behaviour.

Added to this, the demanding realities of parenting and trying to make a living interfere with this attachment process by keeping the spouses apart for long periods during the day and by introducing stress into their lives. The combination of the end of the powerful romantic love feelings with the stresses of life causes many relationships to deteriorate into bickering and the development of separate lives. Divorce often results.

Most divorces, then, are not the result of physical abuse or addiction to drugs, alcohol, or gambling, but instead come from the feeling that the love has gone out of the relationship and from the arguing and disagreements that follow. The disappointment that occurs when those intense feelings of the early days fade is interpreted by many as the disappearance of all emotions from the relationship. When this occurs, most people do not have the communication skills to be able to discuss their fears and concerns, to resolve their differences, and subsequently to find a way to rekindle their original affection. It is a major failing in our society that conflict resolution skills are not taught anywhere in the education system. As a result, the disappointed feelings slowly change to anger and frustration.

The emotions that accompany this marital dissatisfaction are usually so strong that it is impossible to carry on a reasonable discussion, as the anger and frustration enter every conversation almost immediately and suddenly both parties are shouting at each other. These continued disagreements when trying to resolve the problems just confirm that the marriage is over and, without third-party intervention in the form of marriage counselling, often result in divorce.

When the cause of the marital dissatisfaction is clearer, such as abuse by one spouse, the addiction of a marital partner, or the persistent infidelity of one of the partners, negative feelings are considerably stronger. The injured party feels betrayed, angry, and sometimes even guilty that he or she may have in some way caused their spouse's behaviour. The guilty partner may not clearly understand his or her role in the breakdown of the marriage, or, due to strong emotional defences, not even accept responsibility for them and so not want the divorce. This person is then left with intense feelings of anger, often based on guilt, over the fact that the divorce is proceeding.

No matter the cause of the marital breakdown, the fact that most marriages break down under conditions of anger and frustration is what leads to the development of what could be termed "breakup baggage." Occasionally one hears of "amicable divorces" where both parties in the marriage agree to go their separate ways and manage to do so without negative feelings toward the spouse. Unfortunately these are few and far between. Instead, one or both of the marriage partners usually ends up with a mixture of these negative feelings that constitutes the breakup baggage. These powerful negative feelings subsequently interfere with the divorce settlement, including custody arrangements if there are children, and often continue for years after the actual separation of the partners so that future relationships are also affected.

The Nature of Breakup Baggage

Breakup baggage has its origin in what is basically a grief reaction. Grief generally results from a loss of some kind. Usually this is associated with the death of a loved one, but it can also result from the loss of a valued job or the loss of a marriage. The emotions associated with grief vary and several stages to this process have been identified. For example, Elizabeth Kubler-Ross, in her groundbreaking book *On Death and Dying*, identified five stages of grief, which were actually emotional stages that she perceived in those diagnosed with a terminal illness. The stages Kubler-Ross identified are:

Denial: "This isn't happening to me!" or
                   "She'll come back soon."

Anger: "Why is this happening to me?" or
                   "How can he do this to me?"

Bargaining: "I promise I'll be a better person if only she
                   pulls through."

SCOTT WOODING

Depression:	"I don't care anymore."
Acceptance:	"I'm ready to get on with my life."

With the exception of bargaining, which cannot occur after an actual loss, these stages have come to be accepted as common in most grief situations. While there are other theories on the emotions and stages of grief, most authorities and grief counsellors agree that the feelings associated with this process include the following:

Shock or numbness	Denial
Anger	Guilt
Depression	Acceptance

The behaviours associated with these emotions initially include crying, anger outbursts, sleeplessness, fatigue, loss of appetite, and concentration problems. If not properly resolved, they often harden into anger and bitterness. These emotions do not necessarily come in a particular order, with the exception of acceptance, which, it is to be hoped, is the final stage, and the feelings are not all experienced by everyone, but the majority of them are definitely part of most marital breakdowns.

The main culprits that interfere in the resolution of a divorce and that can then go on to interfere with future marriages are anger and guilt. These powerful feelings come from several sources. Many spouses are angry if they feel that it is not their fault that the marriage is ending or if they did not want it to end, even if their behaviour has been a major part of the problem. Others become enraged that their partner has had the nerve to walk out on them, once again, regardless of the role their behaviour played in the process.

Guilt is often generated by the sense of failure that results from marital breakdown. Our culture teaches that marriages are supposed to be forever, so that when they end prematurely some people experience guilt, on the assumption that they could have done more to save the marriage. This same guilt can come from the disappointment displayed by relatives and children that the relationship did not last and the resultant feeling that they have been let down.

If these feelings exist in one or both of the previous marital partners, they are likely to have serious effects on future relationships. In fact, these effects are often so drastic that they can destroy the new partnership. It is worthwhile to examine these emotions in order to understand why they can be so harmful and how to avoid their intrusion into a new relationship.

Anger

Anger is an emotion characterized by aggressive, explosive energy. It is an ancient emotion that probably evolved to save people's lives by giving them the strength and energy necessary to defend themselves. Thus, the purpose of anger appears to be to energize people to deal with enemies, and to overcome life-threatening obstacles. The process starts inside two almond-shaped structures in the brain called the *amygdala*. The amygdala is responsible for identifying threats to human well-being, either physical or mental, and for sending out an alarm to the body when these threats are identified. This then results in people taking steps to protect themselves.

This protection mechanism is complex and immediate. When a potential threat is recognized by the amygdala, neurotransmitter chemicals known as *catecholamines* are instantly released. These chemicals are mainly *adrenaline* and *noradrenalin*. Their effect is to cause the muscles to tense up and the heart rate to go up to 180 beats per minute or even higher, compared to the regular heart rate, which averages about 80. The blood pressure, too, goes up, to 220/130 or even higher, compared to the normal readings of 120/80. The body also uses up sugar extremely fast to fuel the burst of energy, creating a sugar deficiency. As a result, the person often shakes in anger. Breathing rates increase to get more oxygen into the bloodstream and perspiration begins to cool what is expected to be an overheated body from the exertion of defending itself. The body is immediately ready to fight the enemy.

The reality of the world of today is that most of the perceived threats do not involve being attacked by enemies or wild animals, and rarely involve life-threatening circumstances that need all this physiological arousal. Instead, the threats are mostly psychological, including angry bosses, rude clerks, snarled traffic, and contrary spouses. Rather than a physical response, these modern stressors require thought and analysis to deal with them. Unfortunately, this cannot happen once the anger response has been invoked. Since it was imperative in the days of warring tribes and vicious wild animals to respond immediately to the attack, the mechanism by which the amygdala responds to these perceived threats does not utilize the cortex, which is the thinking part of the brain. Instead it sends its chemical messengers directly to the parts of the body that are necessary to make the person stronger and faster. The angry person's attention then narrows and becomes locked onto the target of the anger, shutting out all other stimulation.

The result is that the angry person reacts rather than thinks. All focus is on defending against the perceived threat or on attacking and hurting it. Since physical action is rarely possible in modern society, angry words, threats, and insults are used instead. This is unfortunate because rarely can this approach succeed in solving a problem. Rather, the other person perceives it as a threat, and his or her anger mechanism kicks in. The result is an angry confrontation rather than a solution to the problem.

Another problem with the anger response is that it takes time for this emotion to wind down. Once the target of the anger is no longer accessible or an immediate threat, people start to return to their relaxed state. However, this process is relatively slow compared to how quickly the anger response is triggered. The arousal state created by the anger can last for several hours, during which time the person has a lowered anger threshold, making it easier to get angry during this wind-down stage. An angry confrontation with the boss during the day can then lead to yelling at the kids for minor infractions when the person gets home.

A clear example of the effects of anger in separation situations was shown by John, an alcoholic whose wife Mary had left him two years earlier. He displayed his anger about the situation in many ways, such as by refusing to change weekends with the children if Mary had a special event to attend, and by being constantly late in picking up and delivering the kids on his weekends. However, his most damaging angry reaction to the situation was to call Child Protection and complain that Mary and her boyfriend were physically abusing the children (which they were not). The subsequent investigation took weeks and left Mary and her boyfriend terrified to discipline the children for fear that they would be taken away. John took this action purely out of anger at his situation for the purpose of upsetting and harassing his ex-wife. Unfortunately this type of action is all too common in the battles that surround situations where breakup baggage exists. _____

When one or both former spouses are angry about the termination of the relationship, nothing good can happen. This baggage usually takes years to unload, and in that time period everyone involved will experience considerable anguish. Anger has no place in today's world. It can only be destructive, as that's how the mechanism developed. When children are involved, it is vital that the cognitive part of the brain be used and not the anger mechanism so they are not drawn into the battle and hurt by the fallout from it.

Guilt

Guilt is a much more complicated emotion than anger as it can display itself in so many ways, most of which are either self-destructive or destructive to ex-spouses and their families. It is both a mental and an emotional experience that occurs when a person realizes that he or she has violated a moral standard and is responsible for that violation. The result is conflict and emotional distress as to how to resolve this very powerful feeling.

Unlike anger, the neural mechanism of guilt has not been identified. Many theorists believe that guilt is a learned response that results from the teachings of parents and society. Others postulate that guilt is actually an evolutionary mechanism that has developed to reduce the violence in society. The theory is that if a person feels guilty when he or she physically or emotionally harms another, that person is more likely not to harm others or become too selfish in the future. Whatever the origin and purpose of guilt, it is a powerful emotion that can have major effects on future relationships.

This is especially true if guilt results from marital breakdown. If one of the former partners believes that he or she was responsible for the breakup, or did not do enough to resolve the marriage problems, then a range of emotions can be displayed. One is depression, which manifests itself in feelings of worthlessness and despair. Typically a person experiencing these feelings would just want to get the divorce over with, not want much from a settlement, and would just fade away from the former spouse. If children are involved, the depressed person might even fade away from their lives. This, however, is not the typical pattern the guilty person follows.

More common is that the guilty feelings gradually change form, moving from feelings of worthlessness to anger at oneself. This is often called remorse. Unfortunately, the human mind does not easily accept this inward anger and works to protect the person from himself or herself. To do this, the mind changes the feelings once again to resentment for the remorse. It then vents the remorse on something—or somebody—else, generally the person who is deduced to have caused the guilt in the first place. As the resentment grows, it turns into full-fledged anger against the person who has been hurt, anger because that person has made the guilty one feel so bad. Amazingly the cycle does not always stop there, but can repeat itself endlessly if no help is obtained.

This repetition is caused by the expressions of anger toward the nonoffending person, resulting in even more guilt as, subconsciously, the angry person—the one who caused the breakup in the first place—feels more guilt for being angry. This starts the cycle all over again. Since this can be rather confusing to imagine, it is diagrammed below.

Guilt-Anger Cycle

- *Guilt*: from causing the marriage breakup
- *Remorse*: for hurting the former spouse and children
- *Anger at Self*: for hurting former spouse
- *Resentment*: toward former spouse for having caused the anger
- *Anger*: at former spouse for causing these feelings

This guilt-anger cycle helps to explain some of the more puzzling instances of breakup baggage. These are the ones when one party is very clearly the cause of the marital termination, yet that person is the angriest and the one who displays the most childish behaviour. As an illustration, the case of Kurt and Josie is typical:

While the 12-year marriage had included its share of fighting and disagreements, Josie was stunned when suddenly Kurt announced he was leaving. They had recently gone through a difficult period financially while building a new house—a house that had been Kurt's inspiration—but this period seemed to be over. Josie was even more hurt when the almost 40-year-old Kurt immediately moved in with a 19-year-old colleague from work. Josie understandably went into a depression, while Kurt equally as quickly started to be antagonistic toward her—mainly with regard to the custody arrangements for their nine-year-old daughter, but also about the financial support for mother and daughter. This antagonism showed itself in Kurt's refusal to communicate with Josie, his refusal to be flexible about visitation weekends, and his refusal to pay any child or spousal support. A court battle quickly developed over both custody and finances, which only increased Kurt's anger.

The question on most people's minds would be, "What has Kurt got to be angry about?" After all, he was the one who walked out on his wife and daughter and moved in with a girl half his age. The answer can clearly be found in the guilt-anger cycle. While he was clearly in love with his new girlfriend, he knew that leaving his wife and family for another woman was wrong. The guilt generated by this knowledge quickly followed the change to remorse, then to inward anger at the conflicting feelings he was experiencing. At this point, his mental defensive mechanisms automatically started up and this inward anger was blocked, turning into anger toward the person he felt had caused these conflicting feelings. Suddenly, he was angry with his wife.

This process occurred over a very short period of time and was almost entirely subconscious. In the space of just a few weeks, Kurt came to really believe that it was his former spouse who was the cause of his problems. His defence mechanisms were so strong that he also refused to believe that his nine-year-old daughter would be upset with his behaviour. He assumed that she would be happy to visit him and his girlfriend and would understand his behaviour. This was far from the case. Even a nine-year-old can figure out what really happened when confronted with a stranger living with her father and the genuine grief that her mother was experiencing.

The grief-anger cycle also often occurs with physical or emotional abuse. The abuser clearly knows that the marriage broke up because of his or her behaviour and normally feels guilty about it. Once again, guilt feelings are unacceptable and the cycle develops. The abuser becomes angry with the spouse for making him or her become abusive. Outsiders are baffled by the abuser's anger as they see that the cause of the breakup was clearly that person's behaviour. Unfortunately, the abuser cannot see this, and the angry behaviour that originally caused the marriage to end continues into the post-marital period as breakup baggage.

The feelings that result from the grief of a broken relationship all too often result in breakup baggage that goes on to affect the relationship of the former partners for years to come. When grief results in depression in one of the partners, that person can be virtually paralyzed for long periods of time. The depression causes them to not be able to act effectively, at work or in the home. In many cases of depression, one or more of the children has to take over many of the parent's functions because he or she (in most cases it is she, as the mother usually gets the majority custody) is incapable of doing them. When the grief results in guilt or anger, then any process that needs to involve the two people can be protracted and rancorous.

This is particularly true when kids are involved. In these cases, which make up the majority of divorces, the two parents are linked forever by a biological relationship. Both are parents of the children and so, no matter how their respective lives move forward, this link will continue to exist. If there is a considerable amount of breakup baggage, then all decisions and actions that involve the children will be, at best, strained and difficult and, at worst, impossible. By far the most dangerous aspect of this breakup

SCOTT WOODING

baggage is that the stress it creates often goes on to affect any new relationships, and even to eventually destroy them.

The Manifestation of Breakup Baggage

When strong negative emotions result from the breakup of a relationship, this baggage can show itself in many ways. Several have been mentioned above, but there are an almost infinite number of methods that an angry or guilty ex-spouse can use to display these emotions. The topics below include many of the main signs of breakup baggage.

Money

One of the clearest signs of an emotional hangover from the ending of a relationship is strict control of money. Usually this tactic is employed by the male as he often is either the only breadwinner or the main breadwinner in the family and only rarely has primary custody of the children. However, money can be a weapon for either partner, depending on the circumstances.

This tactic can start with emptying bank accounts or stripping companies of their assets, and has been known to go so far as a person quitting his job so as to have less available money. These are drastic measures that can obviously be harmful to the person using them in terms of their careers and earning potential, but it is indicative of how far angry people will go to thwart their former mates.

Lesser monetary controls include refusing to pay school fees, or for extracurricular activities, summer camps, or even therapy for the children. Each payment above the amount the angry ex-spouse has grudgingly agreed to pay monthly is extracted with great difficulty, if at all, creating endless battles and angry confrontations. Money makes an excellent weapon and angry people are very willing to use this to vent their frustration.

Harassment and Intimidation

Basically these are bullying tactics easily employed by either of the ex-partners to exact revenge on the other. These tactics include frequent angry phone calls and e-mails about real or imagined slights from the former spouse, stalking and spying and harassing ploys through the ex's lawyer. The telephone calls can often include crude and threatening language as well as shouting and cursing. Stalking and spying are self-explanatory but few people realize how frightening they are to the person being stalked. They form an incredibly effective power ploy. The legal approach includes bringing every disputed point to court, often knowing that the former partner cannot afford the frighteningly high lawyer's bills.

Another harassment method is calling up cellular telephone records on the computer to determine who the ex-spouse is calling, then using this information in various ways. This could include calling the people on the list to warn them against associating with the former spouse or just letting the ex know that their life is being monitored—in effect another stalking technique. These records should not be available to the former partners, but somehow they can often get them.

These tactics are childish, but those affected by breakup baggage rarely are able to examine their own behaviour. An amazing amount of time and energy that could better be expended in rebuilding the harasser's life is spent on such vengeful activities. Instead, these people are far more intent on hurting their ex-spouse than in stopping long enough to see what benefit this behaviour is actually bringing to them.

YOUR EX-WIFE IS ON LINE ONE

Rob could almost set his watch by his ex-wife Marion's calls. Each day around 10:00 AM she would be on the phone to him, angrily complaining about something real or imagined that Rob had done to her. After enduring weeks of these calls, he

SCOTT WOODING

started telling the switchboard operator that he was not in. This resulted in Marion dictating angry and embarrassing messages for him that would dutifully be placed in his inbox each day. To avoid these messages, he asked the operator to tell Marion that he would not take her calls. This resulted in such a storm of abuse to the poor woman that Rob was soon forced to abandon this tactic as well. Being out of town did not help, as she would phone him on his cell as well. All this despite the fact that Marion had primary custody of the children and he regularly paid his child support. The harassment only stopped after Rob, on the advice of his therapist, calmly answered each call with the statement "I'll only talk to you about issues concerning our children and I'll only discuss these if you are calm and rational." If she did not follow these instructions he simply hung up. Rob's consistent calmness and control was the answer. When it became clear that he was no longer upset by these calls, Marion gave up. ⸺⸺⸺⸺⸺⸺⸺⸺⸺⸺

The Children as Weapons

No tactic resulting from breakup baggage is as despicable as using the children as a weapon in the spousal wars. This is accomplished in several ways. One is to use them to carry messages to the ex, rather than doing it personally. These messages are often angry and abusive ones that the children are embarrassed to carry. It also usually means that the ex-spouse will not communicate in other ways. Examples would be: "Tell your father he's late with his support cheque again," or "Tell that witch that she should be on time next week." This tactic puts the children on the front lines of the war, making them painfully aware of the anger between their parents.

Children are also often used as spies to report on the activities, particularly the amorous ones, of the ex-spouse. This puts the children in a very uncomfortable position as they usually realize that they are being questioned so that one parent can use the information against the other. Unfortunately, children feel powerless against this tactic as they want to please their parent and they often fear that parent's wrath if they refuse to tell tales. While it may be natural to wonder how the other parent is progressing in their love life, it is extremely unfair to place children in this position.

Another use of the children is to refuse to be flexible when it comes to the custody arrangements. If mom needs to change weekends because of a course that she needs to take, dad may refuse in order to complicate her life by having to make alternate arrangements. If dad can't get his holidays when he planned and asks the mother to change his summer weeks so that he can take the children camping, mom may refuse just to inconvenience the father. As petty as this tactic is, it happens all the time

An even more odious way of using the children as a weapon is to actively and obviously denigrate the ex-spouse to the children. This tactic is designed to win the children over to whichever parent is employing it. This involves complaining to the children about the ex, pointing out the former partner's flaws, and telling highly biased versions of why the marriage broke up.

Most of the tactics involving using the children as weapons will usually backfire, as when the kids get into their teens they will be able to see through the angry spouse's behaviour. Still, it frightens and confuses the children when they are young and places them under considerable stress.

Passive Resistance

While this tactic is not as explosive and angry as the previous ones, it is equally as frustrating. It involves the spouse with baggage not doing what is asked, required, or has been promised, but not calling or emailing to say that it will not be done. This could happen if one parent asks the other to pick up the children at a certain time and the spouse never shows up. Another example would be if the baggage-laden was asked to pay for a special event, agreed, then never actually did so. It could also involve just a refusal to communicate, without ever discussing the reasons behind this bizarre behaviour. Thus phone calls are not answered, voicemails are not returned, and emails are ignored.

The reason for this passive approach could be that the ex-spouse employing it was a helpless, disorganized person, but it is more likely that it is a form of anger that avoids immediate confrontation. The passive-aggressive spouse would rather deliver excuses to explain this behaviour later than blatantly refuse to accommodate the former partner at the time.

While some employ one type of tactic consistently, others combine several of the approaches to vent their anger on their former partner. No matter what noxious form of harassment is employed, it is important to realize that much of this baggage-driven behaviour is subconscious in origin. Rarely do any of these guilt-ridden or angry people have any sort of master plan to frustrate their ex. Similarly, they seldom plan any of the individual incidents that they orchestrate. This does not make any of the behaviour less offensive, frustrating, or threatening, but it does help in dealing with it—as will be discussed later in this chapter.

The Effect of Breakup Baggage

It is obvious that the tactics employed by those suffering the effects of breakup baggage will seriously affect the life of the non-warring spouse. Lack of money caused by the refusal of the former partner to pay his or her fair share, constant arguments, being physically or emotionally harassed, or just being ignored all make daily existence miserable for the other parent. While these tactics gravely affect the lives of single parents, they can be even worse for those who have moved on with their lives and have new partners.

The tension created by the baggage-laden ex-spouse can have several effects on new relationships, depending on how the latest partners react to the situation. The main effect is to create a barrier between the partners that results from the tension that one of them is under. The natural tendency when under stress is to vent the aggravation on whoever is close and safe. In other words, the spouse under stress often takes the frustration out on the new partner and the children because they are in the home and because they are unlikely to return the emotion—in contrast to the ex-spouse. Unless more appropriate outlets are found, which is unlikely if counselling is not obtained, this situation is extremely dangerous to the new relationship. A new partner can take the aggravation for a while, but since he or she did not create the problem, this patience is usually limited. This can doom the relationship if no solution is found.

Another result of the tension created by breakup baggage is completely opposite to the above. Since these new partners love and respect their mates, then, out of sympathy and concern, they often throw themselves into these domestic battles, usually with disastrous results. Some merely fuel the flames by coaching their new partner in counter tactics. Rather than helping, this usually makes things worse, as meeting angry tactics with similar ones just results in escalation. Even worse are those new partners who take the lead in the fight. These people insist on answering the phone and blasting the former mates, devise ways to get them back for their baggage tactics, and even adopt harassing techniques of their own. Again, not only does this do nothing to solve the situation, it tends to keep the battles going for years.

The biggest losers in these escalated battles are the children. They cannot help but be aware of the situation, and since they almost always love both biological parents, they too become caught up in the situation. The worst part for them is that they are helpless to do anything about the situation, as usually no one listens to them. Watching their parents battle, even if only one parent is fighting, is painful and frustrating for them. Their helplessness just increases their tension so that anger and depression can often become part of their lives as well.

Resolving Breakup Baggage

There are three important steps to the proper resolution of the powerful emotions that accompany the dissolution of a relationship. These steps include recognition that breakup baggage really exists, finding emotional support to resolve these powerful emotions, and, finally, negotiating a new relationship with the ex-spouse. The first is actually the hardest for many people. It involves the recognition that the person really is going through a grief process and may have some breakup baggage. Many people either downplay the effects of these emotions or actually refuse to believe that they are having them. Those in this latter category are often the ones whose behaviour is the most destructive. They subconsciously employ defence mechanisms such as denial to block out any thoughts that their behaviour may be inappropriate or hurtful to others. These defence mechanisms are incredibly powerful and are so poorly understood by most people that they require explanation in order for people involved in the breakdown of a relationship to be able to move on with their lives.

The Nature and Recognition of Defence Mechanisms

Defence mechanisms are employed subconsciously by the mind as protection from thoughts or feelings that cannot be tolerated. In other words, they protect us from the anxiety and worry produced by thinking that we may be wrong in some way. The defence only allows the unconscious thought or feeling to be expressed indirectly in a disguised form; it does not allow the person employing it to know that he or she is doing this. How these defences developed or where in the brain they are controlled is not currently known. What is understood is that everyone employs them to some extent.

It is interesting that there is a relationship between people's emotional maturity and the sort of coping methods they employ. Less emotionally mature people tend to prefer rather primitive and often inefficient coping methods, while those who are more mature mainly employ more sophisticated and useful methods. The less mature methods also tend to have in common that they are reactive, not well thought out, and the person using them is completely unaware of doing so.

These defence mechanisms are considered to be primitive because they rely on blatant misrepresentation or outright ignorance of reality in order to function. They thrive in situations (and minds) where emotion overrides reason and impulsive behaviour is common. Children use them naturally and normally, but then again, children are emotionally immature, without the experience and learning of adults. When adults use these methods on a regular basis, it is an indication that their emotional development is incomplete. There are several of these mechanisms, and although most people are aware that they exist, few realize that they are using them. They include:

- **Denial**—an outright refusal or inability to accept some aspect of reality that is upsetting. For example: "The marriage breakup was not my fault."
- **Projection**—a thought or emotion about another person, place, or thing is too troubling to admit, consequently that thought or emotion is attributed to the other person, place, or thing. For example: "She caused the breakup," when actually the projecting person was the main cause. Another form of this defence mechanism is known as *externalization*. In externalization, others are blamed for the problems in order to avoid acknowledging any role that the person might have had in causing them. For example: "My mother-in-law interfered in the marriage and caused the breakup."
- **Passive-aggression**—a thought or feeling is not acceptable enough to a person to act on directly. Instead, that person behaves in an indirect manner that expresses the thought or emotion. For example: Agreeing to do things for the ex-spouse, then simply not doing them.

20   SCOTT WOODING

- **Acting out**—an inability to consider the ramifications of impulse. The impulse is expressed directly without any reflection or even consideration that the behaviour is unfair or inappropriate. For example: harassing tactics against the ex-spouse.

The main point to emphasize about these behaviours, which, viewed objectively, are childish, is that they are unconscious. The mind has an incredible ability to protect itself from anxiety and uses these mechanisms to ensure that none is experienced. The anxiety in marriage breakdown usually comes from guilt and the anger that it produces. Since it is intolerable to be angry with oneself, these mechanisms are used to reduce any anxiety that would otherwise be produced.

The fact that these tactics are developed subconsciously makes it difficult for the person utilizing defence mechanisms to realize that he or she is doing so and to stop. This is the main reason that the worst offenders never seem to resolve their anger. They can't unless someone that they trust and respect is able to point out to them the origins of their behaviour, or unless they reach an emotional crisis point of some sort and are forced to examine their own behaviour. This is often called "hitting bottom." These people cannot resolve their breakup baggage until they understand where their feelings are coming from and that they need to move on to the next step.

Those not experiencing anger and guilt have much less difficulty acknowledging their feelings, as they are mainly dealing with helplessness and depression. These feelings do not normally get masked by defences, but they can cause a person experiencing them to feel that their problems are not significant enough to ask for help. No matter how insignificant the separating person thinks these feelings are, help should be obtained to resolve them. If this does not happen, the feelings could worsen and interfere with the ability to deal with day-to-day living in the future.

Unfortunately, few people can deal with their breakup baggage on their own. Couples in the process of breaking up need to understand that strong emotions will be part of the process and that they should immediately take steps to deal with them. They need to move on to the next stage in the process, which is getting emotional support.

Emotional Support

The breakdown of a marriage never occurs without some emotional fall-out. While this can be mild and temporary in cases where there are no children and both parties have agreed that the marriage is not working, there are always some emotions produced. These come from a sense of failure that the marriage could not be made to work, and often from a feeling that something could have been done to fix the situation. Despite the present high rate of divorce, most people do not feel good about having to undergo one.

In those cases where children are involved and where the breakup has been rancorous, the emotions are so powerful that few can resolve them on their own. Even close friends rarely can help, as they are not usually able to be completely objective. Instead, one of two approaches is necessary. Either both parties need to enter into counselling with a qualified practitioner (although not the same one for both), or they need to join separate support groups, also led by qualified persons. Once it is recognized that the emotions caused by the breakup are interfering with their lives, the participants should immediately start looking for one of these solutions.

Finding a good counsellor is not always easy. There are many different counselling styles and counsellor personalities, and not all might be comfortable for the client. The process should be similar to finding a good medical doctor. It starts with searching the Yellow Pages or asking others who have undergone divorce whom they utilized. Asking what credentials the person has is also necessary and reasonable, as not all counsellors are trained in dealing with the aftermath of relationship failure. There are special qualifications beyond just the academic degrees and, while these do not guarantee that the counsellor will be right for you, they do mean that he or she will have the knowledge and experience necessary to do the job.

The next step is to see if that person will be right for you. One visit to a counsellor does not lock you into a future with him or her. Just as you would not stay with a poor mechanic, there is no point in continuing to pay a counsellor you are not comfortable with. It is easy to tell if the counsellor is the right one. If you feel relaxed and comfortable talking to the person, if the advice given seems reasonable and logical, and if you leave each session feeling better than you felt when you went in, then the right counsellor has been selected.

A good counsellor will explore the causes of the breakup and try to explain the origin of your feelings. He or she will then outline acceptable ways of dealing with the guilt, anger, or depression that is being experienced. The modern approach is to try to change the client's "self-talk," which is defined as our mindset, attitudes, internal dialogue, or inner belief systems. Normally this is not a lengthy process. The days of lying on a couch and word-associating for years have long since gone. Instead, the process can normally be accomplished in six to eight sessions, although it could be more in very serious situations.

Support groups can also be very effective. These are normally run by churches, community organizations, individual counsellors, or they can be government sponsored. While often harder to find than counsellors, they can be discovered through newspaper advertisements, through ministers and pastors, and by calling local help lines. These groups work by gathering people in similar circumstances who then discuss the feelings they are experiencing and the solutions they have found. It is a communal approach to breakup baggage that is usually cheaper than individual counselling and that helps a person to realize that he or she is not alone in their emotions. The group approach might not be for shy people, although the groups are almost always very supportive, and it might be a slower process than individual counselling as everyone in the group needs a chance to speak. Nevertheless, support groups are usually very helpful in the process of reducing breakup baggage, and they have the advantage of providing something of a social life for the newly single participants.

No matter how intense the feelings may seem after a breakup, some form of counselling should be sought immediately. Defence mechanisms quickly mask many of the feelings, and the damage created by breakup baggage can begin.

Negotiating the New Relationship

Once the breakup baggage has been resolved to a point where both parties can act rationally, often at least a six-month process, it will be possible to negotiate the outline of a new relationship with the ex-partner. In the emotional climate of the original breakup, many temporary arrangements may have been made that, seen in a baggage-free light, might not have been practical. For example, many distraught refugees from a bad relationship will make statements such as, "I don't want anything from him/her, I just want out." When reality sets in, it can easily be seen that this is unrealistic and unfair. Similarly, many leave their relationships without resolving custody arrangements for the children. As will be discussed later, this can have disastrous effects on the future relationship with the children. Once the strong emotions associated with the original breakup are out of the way, it is time to settle all the issues that could not be resolved earlier.

The Process

The first issue that has to be decided is how to accomplish the negotiation. If all the baggage is indeed out of the way, then this can be done in a simple, face-to-face meeting or, more likely, a series of meetings. No intermediary would be necessary. While this is the ideal, it is probably not going to happen very often, as this process requires a maturity and calmness that is difficult, even without the breakup baggage.

Probably the most effective alternative to the do-it-yourself approach is that of mediation. In this method a mediator, often a retired judge or lawyer with considerable experience in the legal field, is hired by both participants to find solutions to the major issues. The mediator's objectivity can save time and money, even after the fees are paid, as discussions can be kept on track and emotions that could otherwise taint the negotiation can be limited. Once an agreement on all major issues is reached, it can be written into a separation agreement or into the divorce agreement itself.

A second approach is that of collaborative law. In this method each side appears at the negotiation table with his or her own lawyer and proceeds to find a solution to the main concerns. If an agreement is reached in this way, then once again it is written into the separation or divorce settlement. While this approach can work well, the disadvantage is in the potential for confrontation between the two lawyers. When there is only a mediator present, this cannot occur, but many people are not sure they can trust one person to truly give them a fair deal, and prefer to have their own representative present. This has the potential to take longer, but the lawyers who do this kind of work usually try to avoid confrontation. If an agreement cannot be reached under this approach and the case has to go to court and be settled by a judge, these lawyers drop out and trial lawyers must be hired.

It must be emphasized that taking the settlement to a judge is not negotiation and probably indicates that all the breakup baggage has not been resolved. Going to court is incredibly expensive and there are no guarantees as to how the problem issues will be resolved. Judges tend to have their own opinions on what is fair and unfair and these may not jibe with your own. Negotiation is a far better and cheaper approach, but it means that there must be give and take on such crucial issues as finances and custody. Participants cannot go into any of these processes expecting to get everything their way. There are two sides to every issue and it takes a calm, mature person to realize this.

Finances

It depends on the situation, but usually the first issue that needs to be solved is the financial settlement. Joint property needs to be split up and support payments, both child and spousal, need to be set. Each state and province has its own laws to cover many of the major property issues so that this aspect should be reasonably straightforward. However, the smaller items, such as the painting that Aunt Mary gave as a wedding present and the dishes that were purchased jointly with wedding money, are often more sensitive issues. Whenever there is sentimental value attached to an item, then its disposition can be difficult. This is where a sense of fairness and a certain amount of objectivity are required. It is amazing to see a couple wrangling over a set of salt-and-pepper shakers that are worth just a few dollars, but it happens all the time. They are just objects and not worth the hassle, no matter what sentimental value they might have. The important thing is to keep the objective in mind. That is the clinical separation of the marriage and not the sense of triumph that may come with winning possession of some tiny object.

Support payments have long been a major source of contention in marriage breakups. These usually only come into play when children are involved. Once again it takes maturity and a sense of fairness to set these payments so that both sides are content. To do this, both parties must get rid of any concept of winning and losing; the idea that "I'm going to take that (expletive deleted) for all I can get!" just won't work and you could easily end up in court. Instead it is vital that all baggage be left at home and an amount that is reasonable for both sides be set. If there *is* a real "winner" in this process—that is, if one side gets considerably more than the other was willing to pay—the resentment that follows will colour the relationship for years. Since when children are involved the former partner is never completely out of your life, it only makes sense not to try to "win" and to avoid the anger that will inevitably result if you do.

The negotiation process should be fairly simple when it comes to setting support payments as it mainly involves facts. These include:

- How much does each spouse make?
- How much money is needed for the children each month?
- What are the fixed payments that each spouse needs to make each month?

Honesty here is the key factor and that, once again, requires maturity to achieve. The aim of this process is not to hurt the other person, but to decide what is a reasonable amount required to raise the children. Since the children belong to both parents, then both parents should be motivated to see that they are provided for. To do otherwise is to be caught up in the "winning" game, and this does not have the children's welfare in mind.

After this major issue has been settled, it may also be necessary to make decisions about periodic expenditures that may arise concerning the children. These include school fees, camp tuition, music and other types of lessons, prom dresses, and many, many more. Since these cannot all be anticipated, a process should be agreed upon to negotiate these future expenditures. This is one of the major reasons why separated and divorced parents have to be on cordial terms with each other. If they aren't, then every one of these situations becomes a battle. The result is then stress on both parents—stress that can affect the children and stress that can seriously affect future relationships.

Custody

This is without doubt the most emotionally charged and difficult issue to resolve once a marriage has dissolved. Once again, it often turns into a power struggle. This needs to be avoided at all costs, especially for the sake of the children. Disputes over custody are often so emotionally charged that they seriously affect future relationships by dragging the new partner into the conflict.

Much has been written about what arrangement is most beneficial to the emotional health of the children of divorce. Unfortunately, the research is often equivocal and is open to interpretation. Since the mid-eighties, judges have been leaning toward joint physical custody as a "fair" solution to both parents. A 2002 study by Bauserman, heavily supported by the American Psychological Association, was thought to provide definitive backing for the joint physical custody approach. Unfortunately, it has since been shown to have many procedural flaws (including a very small sample of studies analyzed) and fails to provide the definitive answer to the question of which custody arrangement is best for the emotional health of the children.

A more objective analysis of this issue was provided in a 1999 report by Diane Lye to the Washington State Gender and Justice Commission and Domestic Relations Commission. After reviewing a wide selection of studies on the custody issue, she concluded, "No specific pattern of post-divorce parenting arrangements has been clearly demonstrated to confer greater benefits to children." In other words, the one-size-fits-all court-room approach to awarding joint physical custody may not be the best arrangement in many cases. She identified two factors that complicated the post-divorce parenting process: parental conflict and the consistency of child support payments.

Most psychologists and parenting authorities agree that the more contact children can have with each parent the better. However, Lye indicates that in highly conflicted families, in other words, those with high levels of breakup baggage, any benefits of increased contact between the children and the non-residential parent are likely to be offset by the harmful effects of greater exposure to the conflict between the parents. The danger is that the children become involved in this conflict as messengers, through parental attempts to sway them to one side or the other, or just by witnessing frequent bickering and petty harassing techniques. This affects their emotional health.

Lye also found that when parents pay their child support in full and on time, the children's mental health is improved. This could be because it indicates that the parents are cooperating, at least on this issue. It could also be that payment compliance results in more contact and involvement of the non-resident parent. Whatever the reason, researchers tend to agree that household income is the most important influence on child well-being after divorce.

Despite the volume of research on which form of post-divorce parenting is the most effective, there is still no final answer. However, no matter what arrangement is adopted, most authorities do agree on the following guidelines:

- Live close together. The less disruption involved in moving back and forth between houses, the better for the children. When the parents' houses are close together the school is also close, as are the children's friends.
- Spend as much time as possible with the children.
- Maintain a cordial relationship with the ex-spouse so that both biological parents can attend important events.
- Keep up child-support payments.
- Be flexible. Life is not always predictable and schedules sometimes have to be changed. If one parent cannot stick to the agreed schedule for a good reason, then changes should be made.
- Try to keep approaches to discipline as similar as possible. Different rules and enforcement practices only confuse children. More will be said on this topic in a later chapter.

Negotiating a new relationship is not enjoyable or easy, and it cannot be effectively done without shedding as much of the breakup baggage as possible. The process requires objectivity and common sense. If these attitudes can be adopted, then a fair and equitable settlement can be obtained and there will be significantly less strife between the divorced parents in the future.

Children's Breakup Baggage

Breakup baggage is not always just a parental phenomenon. In many cases children can also be affected with the emotions of guilt and anger. This often occurs when the children are not carefully informed of the reasons the marriage broke up and so draw their own conclusions. Parents often feel they are protecting their children by not giving them any of the details of the breakup, thinking that they will understand at some later date. They either believe that their children were seeing the same things they were and so will be able to accept the breakup of the marriage, or that they are too young to form any opinions of their own. This philosophy is particularly dangerous with children eight years and older, as by this age they are highly capable of drawing their own—often erroneous—conclusions.

One of the most common types of breakup baggage experienced by children is guilt; they believe that they somehow caused the marriage dissolution. They often pick up this idea from overheard fragments of arguments between their parents. If, for example, the argument involves differences in disciplinary approaches, children will often hear their names mentioned. This may be only one of many topics that the gradually estranging parents fight over, but it can be enough to lead the kids to believe that they are causing the problem. The resulting guilt feelings can be very powerful and can often lead to depression.

Depression in children is often hard for parents to diagnose, as it does not appear just as a general sadness and lack of interest in normal activities, but instead often appears as irritability and sleep disturbances. If parents are caught up in their own problems, such as making a living and dealing with the divorce details, they may miss the symptoms entirely. This depression can lead to problems with peers, poor school performance, and even the possibility of suicide. While this latter possibility is remote, depression should not be underestimated. It can have a very powerful effect on children. While parents may suspect that the behaviour results from the divorce, they may not realize that the kids are blaming themselves for the breakup.

SCOTT WOODING

Another common emotion experienced by the children of divorce is anger, specifically resentment that their family has broken up. This may be a perfectly normal reaction if the cause of the breakup is clear, such as an alcoholic or abusive parent. The anger will then be directed at the offending parent. While this emotion is understandable in this circumstance, anger in children must always be dealt with, as it can be as destructive to them as it can be to adults. It is displayed in many different ways, including poor school performance, frequent temper tantrums, or it, too, can result in depression.

Much more destructive to future relationships is anger that is directed at the parent who left the family home because he or she could no longer tolerate the situation. This may not, in fact, be the parent who has caused the marriage to become intolerable, especially since in many cases it is not just one parent's fault. However, if, due to a lack of more complete information, a child draws the conclusion that the parent who left was the one who was responsible for the disintegration of the family, this could drastically affect the future relationship between the child and that parent. This point is illustrated in the following example:

For 15 years Gail was married to Harry. By the time their two kids were entering their teens, Gail could no longer tolerate the relationship. Harry had proven to be a complete control freak. He controlled the money supply down to the nearest penny. He allowed Gail no freedom, making her account for every minute of her time. She was hounded if she spent any time with friends or in recreational activities. They had no friends as a couple and shared no leisure activities. Gail suggested counselling, but Harry consistently refused, seeing nothing wrong with the relationship. Finally, after 17 years, Gail had had enough and found the courage to move out.

Initially, both children came with her and lived in her condominium. Harry quickly obtained a high-priced lawyer and took every detail of the settlement to court. While he did not always get his way, his harassing tactics took their toll on Gail. Being constantly on edge, she began to have difficulty with her two teenagers, especially her 14-year-old son. Gradually he began spending more and more time with his dad. When he returned from each visitation (it was initially a standard sole-custody arrangement) he was belligerent and argumentative. Finally he demanded to live full time with his father and Gail reluctantly acquiesced. Within a short time he would not even take telephone calls from his mother, effectively ending all contact with her.

When Gail finally began seeing a counsellor, the root of the problem was quickly determined. Harry had been telling his son that Gail had caused their breakup, a breakup that he never wanted. Because Gail had never told her children her side of the story, feeling that she should not burden the children with the sordid details of their father's behaviour, and because Gail had moved out of the family home, the son believed Harry and became angrier and angrier with his mother. This anger had been at the root of the rebellious behaviour that the son had been displaying to his mother. By this time, he would not believe Gail if she attempted to tell her side of the story. All she could do was wait and see if time and maturity would help heal the rift between them. The counsellor suggested telling her daughter the truth so that she would not follow the same path. Gail had believed that she should never say anything negative about the father, even if it was the truth, and so paid a very high price for her scruples.

Anger in children resulting from their beliefs about the root causes of the divorce can clearly create serious problems if not prevented. Thus children should be kept informed of the problems in the marriage well before the dissolution. If there is too much emotion from one party to maintain this communication effectively, a counsellor should be employed as early as possible to help the children through this crisis. Without accurate information, children form their own conclusions and the results of these could create serious problems for many years. These problems not only concern the

SCOTT WOODING

relationships between children and parents, but they can also cause serious emotional problems for the children that can last throughout their lives.

When the Ex Will Not Cooperate

Because breakup baggage generally affects both spouses, each must make a genuine attempt to resolve it so that a new relationship can be negotiated and both lives can move forward. Unfortunately this happens all too rarely. More commonly, one spouse cannot move on and displays the behaviours typical of anger and guilt. In this case, life for the more liberated spouse becomes extremely unpleasant. The problem is that each person can only control his or her own behaviour, and no one can change someone who cannot or will not try to resolve the anger and resentment toward the former spouse.

With this fact in mind, the spouse who has put an end to the anger and/or guilt has to get on with his or her life as best as possible. This means that the harassing and spiteful tactics of the ex have to be ignored or worked around whenever they appear—with no retaliation. Wow! What a lot to ask of a person. It is tantamount to asking for sainthood—Mother Teresa would be proud. Nevertheless, this is the only approach that will have a chance of eventually resolving the conflict. Reacting in kind to the anger and childishness will only cause it to escalate.

It's amazing how infantile adults can get when under the influence of these powerful feelings. It was discussed earlier how angry reactions bypass the part of the brain that is responsible for weighing the appropriateness of the thoughts so that they are directly translated into actions. This results in the kind of childish behaviour that is so often exhibited by angry/guilty ex-spouses. When adults allow these feelings to dominate their behaviour, no outside person can modify it until the angry person actually wants to change. It is this realization that supports the notion that retaliation will not work. Giving the same behaviour back will not cause an angry person to recognize its futility, but will be met by an increased fury. Instead, reacting with calmness and maturity will be much more effective. When the angry person finally realizes that their tactics are having no effect, the irate behaviour will eventually die out. Only the most seriously disturbed individuals can keep up a fight all by themselves. While this realization can take a very long time, patience and persistence will usually be rewarded.

One major benefit of not reacting to the anger-based tactics of an ex is that the spouse without the baggage will feel better about him or herself. Allowing oneself to slide back into the post-divorce state, laden with breakup baggage, will only result in more turmoil and anguish. The best approach is to stay above the conflict. This results in a feeling of satisfaction, a feeling that will not exist if retaliatory tactics are employed. At times this may seem like small compensation when weighed against the constant torment created by the former spouse's harassment. Nevertheless, it is much better to feel good about yourself and to cope with the angry tactics than it is to reply in kind. In fact, this approach is a necessary part of getting on with your life. The mature spouses can at least look themselves in the mirror and be pleased with what they see.

When the Baggage Is Gone

Once the breakup baggage has been banished, then the new challenges of life as a single parent can be met much more effectively. These challenges include dealing with finances on your own, parenting the children effectively, maintaining a separate residence, and, eventually, finding a new partner. It's not that a single parent can't deal with these things while under the influence of breakup baggage; it's just that it is much harder. For example, disciplining children while angry and upset is a very dangerous process. All too often the angry parent overreacts, to the puzzlement and frustration of the children, and actually takes out much of their frustration with life on those that they love the most. This is a strange aspect of human nature and very hard on the unsuspecting children. They take these overreactions very seriously and often blame themselves for upsetting the parent, when this is not the problem at all. Parenting is much more balanced when there is little or no breakup baggage left.

Similarly, it is very dangerous to enter into a new relationship before the baggage is resolved. The stress and frustration of dealing with the ex-spouse will affect the new relationship and potentially endanger it. It would take a saint to put up with a constantly stressed person. This does not mean that both ex-spouses necessarily have to have their breakup baggage behind them. This would be nice, but too often it does not happen. However, as long as the person entering a new relationship has his or hers resolved, then they will not be as affected by the continuing belligerence of their ex. This will mean fewer arguments and conflicts in the new relationship and will allow it to run its course naturally. In other words, it may become permanent or it may not, but at least the new person will not have been driven away by the emotions produced by breakup baggage.

The power of breakup baggage should not be underestimated. If not resolved it can create huge problems for many years. It is one of the main reasons that second marriages fail more often than first ones, and it is a major cause of emotional damage to children of divorce. It is vital that it be addressed and resolved if life is ever to get back to normal.

Chapter 2

Dating and Courtship

… thousands of years of human experience and a vast body of contemporary social science research both demonstrate that married husbands and wives, and the children they conceive and raise are happier, healthier, and more prosperous than people in any other living situation. • Peter Sprigg ⸻

Marriage is a popular institution, for which we can all be thankful. It provides a system for children to grow up in a stable emotional and economic environment and for adults to live in an atmosphere of love, companionship, and stability. Despite the recent growth of common-law living, almost 90 percent of adults marry at some time in their lives. As discussed briefly in the introduction, marriages today are difficult to sustain, so the divorce rate in the U.S. is over 50 percent, while in Canada it hovers around the 40 percent mark. Despite this failure rate, a healthy 70 percent of divorced people eventually remarry, indicating the support the institution of marriage continues to maintain.

Unfortunately, in the U.S. about 60 percent of these remarriages also fail. While this failure rate is lower in Canada, the figures clearly show that experience alone is not enough to make a second marriage work. Obviously there are other factors at work of which veteran brides and grooms are unaware. In fact, there are many such factors. The problem appears to be that divorced people are not aware of the issues that conspire to create problems for a second marriage and therefore do not take the appropriate steps to avoid them. This chapter is designed to help newly separated and divorced persons identify the problems associated with reentering the dating arena and to avoid the pitfalls that can lead to a disastrous second marriage.

Getting Reacquainted with Yourself

Resolving the breakup baggage is necessary to reduce the conflict between your ex-spouse and yourself so that you can get on with your life. However, it may not tell you much about why the first marriage failed. It also tells you little about the feelings that have resulted from the divorce that could interfere with a future relationship. This information is necessary in order for you to fully recover from the effects of the first disaster and to avoid similar problems in the future.

Many feelings and emotions resulting from a divorce can create barriers for future relationships. These include:

- Loss of self-confidence. When people entered their first relationship they probably never thought about it failing. Now, after the bitter experience of a failed relationship, many will blame themselves for the failure and worry that there is something wrong with themselves. This leads to self-doubt and possibly . . .
- Fear of failure. With the loss of self-confidence comes an increased concern about ever being able to sustain a relationship. This will certainly interfere with the dating process, either never allowing it to start, or hampering it with fearfulness and timidity.

- Loss of dreams for the future. All the plans and dreams people once had for the future are now radically changed, leading to fear and discouragement that they may ever be reached.
- Loss of support. Where once people had another person in their life to give them support and encouragement, suddenly they are alone to make their own decisions. This loneliness can be frightening and threatening and even dangerous, because it can lead to rebound romance just to have someone, even though the person may not be any more compatible in the long term than the former partner.

In order to avoid having these emotions negatively affect future relationships, two approaches should be considered. The first involves getting some counselling to explore why the first relationship failed. This option is generally rejected by most people due to the cost, the problem of finding a good counsellor, and the continuing stigma that is attached to seeing a "shrink." This rejection is unfortunate because it is extremely difficult to be objective enough to look honestly at your own part in a failed relationship. In fact, most people simply want to blame the former spouse and carry on with their lives. Others may unfairly blame themselves. The fact is that the failure of the great majority of relationships is a two-person problem. Only in the rare cases of abusive relationships and addiction can one person clearly be said to be the one who caused the marriage to fail. In all other cases it was the combination of the two personalities that resulted in the dissolution of the marriage. Certainly there is often more fault attached to one of the partners, but the fact remains that each person had some contribution to make to the demise of the relationship.

Counselling allows a non-involved person to review the relationship and point out the roles played by each person. Not only that, but a good counsellor can show how childhood experiences, both in the home and with peers, affected your first choice of mate. It takes a mature person to be able to listen to their own character flaws and to the mistakes they made in the first relationship. However, if the counsellor is competent, this will be done in a supportive manner. The aim is not to destroy a personality but to make it stronger.

Occasionally a close friend can help to sort out what went wrong in a relationship. However, rare is the friend who can be fully candid. It takes the combination of an open mind on the part of the person from the failed relationship and the ability to be very honest on the part of the friend. If this can be done, then counselling will not be necessary. Usually, though, friends just want to be supportive and to help their comrades through the present crisis period. This often results in having someone who will listen, but who will not offer constructive advice. Counselling is a better option in most cases.

The second approach to preventing the emotions associated with a failed marriage from affecting future relationships is to take some time off from having anything to do with dating or the opposite sex for a while. The first rule should be, "No dating until the divorce is final." The reason for this is that the breakup baggage is strongest during this period and, as discussed in the previous chapter, it will definitely affect the development of a new relationship. Next, there needs to be time to explore the feelings not associated with the breakup baggage but which are nevertheless powerful enough to interfere with a new relationship. Not until a thorough "self-exploration" has been done should any dating be attempted. Many authorities recommend that people wait a minimum of one year after the divorce before resuming their love life. This is not just because of emotions that the divorced person is experiencing, it is also because of the children from a relationship. This will be further discussed, but if kids are involved, the waiting period before resuming dating should probably be more like a minimum of three years.

"If the person you're thinking of dating has been married or you've been, married ... (the) waiting period is one whole year after the divorce has become final. This is such a crucial and

SCOTT WOODING

important point, I'm going to say it again: WAIT ONE FULL YEAR AFTER THE DIVORCE HAS BECOME FINAL. No exceptions."

"It takes time to get out of the trauma, the love, the hate, the guilt, the tears, the sleepless nights, the ex-in-laws, the parents, the best man ... the list goes on and on ..."
• Dr. Joy Browne, *Dating for Dummies*

"Look, the point is that all of us, when something breaks up, want to feel like, 'It wasn't my fault. It wasn't me. I'm the good one.' And the only way we can really do that is for someone else to love us ... The problem is, is that we're still responding from the hangover of the nasty relationship ... 'well, I'll do anything that you need me to do to prove that I'm lovable, because I'm not going to argue. I'm going to be really nice.' And that will last for about six months and then it all hits the fan when we all become who we really are."
• Dr. Joy Browne, radio broadcast, April 8, 2002 ⎯⎯⎯⎯⎯⎯⎯

Widows and Widowers: A Special Case

Divorced persons are not the only ones who suddenly find themselves single and lonely. In many cases the situation has been caused by the death of a partner rather than by a divorce. In such a case the guidelines are similar, but slightly different. Widows and widowers do not have the breakup baggage that usually accompanies divorce, and neither do they have some of the negative emotions after the fact, such as loss of confidence in being able to maintain a relationship. What they definitely do have are grief feelings to deal with—and so do their children. For this reason the waiting guidelines are very similar. The grief must be thoroughly dealt with first before life can move on. Time alone can often heal the wounds caused by the loss, and counselling may not be necessary except in extreme cases. If, after one or two years, either the widowed person's grief or that of the children does not appear to have healed satisfactorily—for example, if one of the children is still suffering from nightmares or enuresis that started after the death—then counselling should be considered.

When the grief has been dealt with, widows and widowers generally experience similar concerns about dating as their divorced counterparts. They have been out of the dating game a long time; life has changed considerably since the widowed person was married and so has the individual. Maturity and experience have changed the person's tastes and interests. Most are no longer interested in the bars and the parties that may have constituted much of their social life before marriage. It takes time to get the confidence to go out, and considerable experimentation to find the best way to meet new people.

"My entire married life was about my husband and my kids. I had no friends of my own, no career, and no hobbies. After he died I needed time to find out who I was. It was about two years before I felt ready to date." • Josie

What to Do While You're Waiting

Many people realize that they are not yet ready to start dating after the divorce; some because they have been out of the singles field for so long and do not feel comfortable with the idea of dating, and others because they are afraid to make another mistake. For these people, waiting until the emotions are dealt with is no problem. Others believe that they should jump right back on the horse after they have fallen off, and so they want to plunge right back into the dating game. These people are so used to doing things as a couple that they are baffled as to how to handle themselves on their own. Many are also lonely and yearn for companionship again, especially if the last few years of the marriage have been ones of turmoil. It is hard for them to imagine living as a single person. The dilemma becomes what to do to remedy these concerns.

While it's not recommended that newly divorced or widowed people begin dating immediately, neither is it recommended that they live the life of hermits, focusing only on their jobs and their parenting. Everyone needs some recreational activities for relaxation and stress relief, especially those who are going through massive lifestyle changes. The idea, then, is to take up some recreational activities that will be enjoyed and that will be relaxing. One approach would be to do some of those things that the person always wanted to do but the former spouse wouldn't. That might involve joining a running club, a bridge group, or a dance troupe. Initially many people, due to some lingering depression or fear of another social failure, will have to force themselves to get out. However, once a toe is in the water, the benefits are great. An added advantage will come when the person is ready to date, since many of these activities involve other single people.

Volunteering is another form of activity that compels single people to interact with others, gets them out of the house, and can be intensely satisfying. In fact, recent research indicates that volunteering is one of the key factors in longevity. This too has the advantage of providing a forum for meeting single people when the time is right.

No matter what activity is chosen, it is vital for a newly single person to "get a life." Naturally this needs to be kept in balance as, with work and parenting, life can be very busy. However, guilt about leaving the kids, if having sole custody is an issue, should not be allowed to hinder this process. Parents not only have a right to some life of their own, but also really need some way to have fun and reduce the effects of the everyday stressors that single-parenting and working produce.

Children Need Adjustment Time, Too

Beyond the many emotional reasons for newly divorced people not to date is an even more important one. As much a shock as the divorce has been for the couple, it is even harder on children. The parents usually could see it coming, but most children are unaware that the breakup is imminent. For this reason, it is vital that they be given time to adjust to the situation.

If the children have been thoroughly informed about the reasons for the breakup of the family, then the emotional impact of the divorce may be lessened. However, no amount of communication will completely eliminate the effects of Mom and Dad no longer being together. Children generally long for their parents to get back together for years after the divorce. The acceptance of this event requires a major emotional adjustment and this will take time. As discussed in the previous chapter, they, too, will normally have a grief reaction that may need counselling support or that will require a lengthy period of adjustment. Adding a new person into this mix at an early stage will not only further confuse the situation, but may cause the kids to blame this stranger for the breakup.

Another adjustment for the children will be the change in residences. The comfortable family home may be gone in the divorce settlement and a new residence, perhaps in a different part of the city, will have to be found. Rarely is the new place as nice as the original family home due to the financial constraints that accompany a divorce. Since Mom and Dad both need a residence, only the wealthiest of families can maintain the same standard of living that they had in the pre-divorce days. This also means that there are two "homes" to get used to and to get comfortable in. This is extremely difficult for children and an adjustment period to this novel situation will be required. This period may be lengthy and, in some cases, may not happen at all in one or other of the residences. Home is usually a comfortable and relaxing place to be, and the new ones may get that way eventually, but until that time the children will not need any more changes in their lives. Dating during this period is definitely not advised.

Along with the change in residences comes the adjustment that the kids will have to make to the dreaded visitation shuffle. The further the residences are apart, the more the disruption, since friends and schools are usually located close to just one of the houses. Younger children can adjust to this constant back and forth fairly well, especially if they enjoy going to both residences. Teens have much more difficulty with this arrangement. They are much more dependent on their friends and resent the disruption to their social lives that the shuffle causes. No matter how much the kids look forward to visiting with each parent, the children need time to get used to the constant travelling between residences. Again, the further disruption that dating would cause is an avoidable complication.

SHUFFLE COMPLICATIONS

The constant shuffle between the separate parental residences is hard enough on children, but many parents make it even more difficult in several ways. The main one is by having different disciplinary standards in the two homes. This is very confusing for children, especially if one home has very little discipline, while the other parent is trying to maintain reasonable standards. Kids can usually adjust, but in some cases this can create huge problems for the parent with higher standards. More will be said on this topic in a later chapter.

Another difficulty is when the non-custodial parent, usually the father, assumes that the children will be happy with just his company and so he makes no attempt to see that they really enjoy their visit. All weekend the kids sit around the condo and watch TV or movies and get bored. If the visit to the non-custodial home is not fun, then the constant drag of having to change residences on a frequent basis will cause the children not to want to come at all. Plans need to be made for enjoyable

activities that the parent and the kids can do together so that
the hardship of the shuffle can be relieved by the fun at the
non-custodial residence. ———————————————————————————

A major impact on the children of divorce that is often overlooked is the
loss of family traditions. Christmas gift opening, Easter egg hunts, and
Thanksgiving turkeys help to give a family its own identity and give children the comfort of belonging to a definable unit. This is very important
to the development of self-confidence in the kids. Once these traditions
are disrupted, new ones must replace them if the children's emotional
growth is to continue. This can prove to be very difficult. Taking Christmas
as the major example, where once there was just one gift-opening ceremony, usually in the family home, now there will be two, often in two new
places. Scheduling these rituals, once trips to the grandparents' homes are
factored into the process, can prove to be very complicated. The logistics
can become a nightmare, further disrupting what used to be a very enjoyable event. This is another major adjustment that children need time to
absorb. It could easily be several years before they get used to the new
ways of doing things.

Another huge adjustment is the difference in standards of living that
often accompany divorce. As mentioned previously, the need for the
divorced couple to maintain two residences, with all their accompanying
costs, significantly impacts the amount of money that is available to them.
One parent, usually the mother, may not have been working before the
divorce and now must find a job to ease the financial burden. This adds
stress and fatigue to this parent, as she is, in fact, maintaining two jobs, at
least while she has the children. While it is certainly possible for the children to get used to these new circumstances, it will, once again, take time.

Newly separated and divorced parents must recognize the difficulty
that children have in making all these major adjustments to their lives.
They do not have the maturity levels that parents normally have, and so
they cannot easily rationalize the emotions that all these critical changes in

their lives bring to the surface. Divorced parents must ensure that the children's needs have been met first before they start to satisfy their own. This is one of the most important reasons for delaying dating for up to several years after the divorce. To do otherwise would be selfish and could do serious damage to the emotional health of the children.

Single-Parenting Habits

One major barrier to the start of dating for divorced parents related to children's adjustment to the situation requires a section of its own. This adjustment involves the habits of interacting with their children that single parents may get into after the breakup. These habits could become a major barrier to future dating if they are not recognized and effectively controlled.

One of these habits involves making one of the children into a confidant. In this circumstance, a lonely and upset newly divorced parent begins to rely on an older child to share his or her concerns and fears. They may also rely on this child to run many aspects of the household. The child often feels very good about this arrangement, as he or she is being treated like a grownup. The problem starts when Mom or Dad begins a new relationship and gradually comes to rely more on the new partner for the emotional support that the child was providing. This can create resentment in the child, who then may begin to sabotage the new relationship. At the very least, the new partner will have a huge barrier to overcome if the relationship should become permanent. The child's resentment about the loss of the adult role will make life very difficult for the newcomer. The child will feel replaced and in his or her own eyes will have become a second-class citizen in a home where he or she was almost an equal partner. In fact, this resentment may never completely die out if not handled correctly.

A classic example of this circumstance was provided by a quiet prairie farmer, Dave, who had been divorced for several years and whose wife had sole custody of their 14-year-old daughter. A farm is a complex operation and so demanded Dave's complete attention. Household details would have been consistently overlooked if it weren't for the weekend visits of Jenny. He relied heavily on her to make shopping lists, help clean the place, and to make decisions on furniture and appliance purchases. All was well with this arrangement until Dave began to go out with Deirdre. After a few months of dating, Deirdre began to spend weekends at the farm, joined by Jenny on her weekends.

At first there did not appear to be any major problems. Jenny would make the odd sarcastic remark, but there were no obvious clashes between the daughter and Dave's girlfriend. The crunch came at a charity event that had been held yearly on Dave's land. Jenny had been a major help in the planning of this event for several years and this year had been no different. Deirdre discovered that, although she was included in the event, she was not seated anywhere near Dave at the final banquet. Jenny was with him the whole time. At the conclusion of the event, Dave and Jenny received the usual thanks from the participants, with no mention of Deirdre. In fact, when pictures were to be taken, Jenny actually pushed Deirdre out of the way so that she could be beside her father. Throughout the day, Dave said nothing to Jenny about her very obvious shunning of his girlfriend. Deirdre's resentment of this treatment became so obvious that a major barrier developed between her and Jenny that even counselling could not break down.

The problem in this situation was not the daughter's behaviour. Jenny was reacting normally to the role that her father had put her in for several years. The real problem was twofold. The first was that it was really Deirdre who needed to understand the situation and be patient with it. A 14-year-old does not have the maturity to see her father's new partner as anything but a threat to the role that he had given her. To expect otherwise

SCOTT WOODING

is to highly overrate a teenager's maturity level. It is up to the adults in the situation to understand what has occurred and take steps to deal with it.

The second problem is that Dave had done nothing to raise Deirdre's profile in the charity event by including her in the planning and by correcting Jenny's plot to exclude her. His hesitancy was also understandable—he was afraid to damage his relationship with his daughter by injecting Dierdre into the process. Dave needed to sit down with Jenny ahead of time and discuss the event and the roles everyone was to play. He also needed to reassure Jenny about his love for her and her importance in his life. By not doing this, he unwittingly was the protagonist in the drama that followed. Dave may also have overestimated Deirdre's capacity to understand the dynamics of his situation and her ability to adjust to it. There was obviously considerable insecurity on Deirdre's part that would need to be addressed as well, as she really should not have been as threatened by Jenny's behaviour as she turned out to be. Unless Dave took the initiative to resolve this situation, either his relationship with his daughter or with his girlfriend would be irreparably damaged.

Leaning on the children, usually the oldest child, for emotional support is understandable, but it places the kids in an unfair position. Many are not emotionally equipped to handle this burden. Others may thrive with the responsibility and the unique relationship that has developed but will be threatened when, inevitably, this role has to change. A new person coming into this situation is then placed in an unfair position that may be almost impossible to resolve. Worse, the child may take their displeasure out on the newcomer, but may actually be mad at the parent. Without counselling intervention this might not be known, so the symptom is treated and not the cause. In other words, the parent may try to improve the child's relationship with his or her new love interest, but actually it is the relationship between parent and child that requires resolution. Parents need to make a conscious effort not to slip into this friendship-like relationship with their children after a divorce. It may provide temporary comfort, but it is a recipe for disaster in the long run.

Another major problem that occurs during single-parenting often occurs with younger children. The trauma associated with a divorce often affects their sleeping habits. They get fearful at night and so want to crawl in with Mommy. The mother often feels guilty about what the divorce has done to the children, so she does not have the heart to say no. However, the difficulty is that once the practice of sleeping with the mother begins, it is very hard to stop. This can be a serious problem at a later date, particularly if remarriage is being contemplated.

The best approach is not to allow it at all. If you are strong enough to do this, there will be fewer weaning problems later and, more importantly, there will not be any significant emotional damage to the child. Unfortunately, this is almost impossible for most parents. Next best would be to make this a time-limited practice. Let the child know that he or she can sleep with Mommy for a week or two, but then has to go back to his or her own bed. This approach must be strictly enforced, no matter how hard it is. The danger of creating a serious dependency is just too great to allow the practice to continue.

Finally, again because of guilty feelings about the divorce, many parents ease up on the rules and consequences of misbehaviour. This is a grave error that can have unfortunate long-term consequences. As will be discussed in greater detail in Chapter 4, discipline is vital in a family to give a child a feeling of safety and security. Knowing where the boundaries are helps children by not forcing them to make decisions about right and wrong. They know what behaviour is expected of them when they have boundaries, and they learn important socialization and respect lessons from receiving consequences for misbehaviour. Parents are doing them no favours by easing disciplinary practices, even though they often think they are.

If changed family circumstances require some new rules or changes in old ones, then that is reasonable. For example, if the new residence is on a busy street, then rules about crossing the street or playing near it may need to be made. However, to dispense with the rules or their enforcement entirely because you feel sorry for the children and their situation is not reasonable. This is true for both custodial and non-custodial parents. Many fathers who do not have primary custody are particularly guilty of this behaviour. If you ever plan to remarry, the consequences of this anarchy will be severe.

HABITS FOR SINGLE PARENTS TO AVOID

- Don't turn your child into a friend or confidant.
- Avoid letting your child sleep in your bed.
- Do not ease up on the family rules. ———————————————————

Let the Dating Begin

The right time to begin dating will vary from person to person, and will depend on the satisfactory resolution of everyone's emotions and a reasonably good adjustment to single life. While the recommended waiting period should be a minimum of one year after the divorce, this is definitely the lower limit. It usually takes several years before both the parents and the kids are ready for the adults to start seeing new people romantically. It should be emphasized that these waiting periods include the non-custodial parent if the situation is one of sole custody. It is often these parents who are ready first, as their lives are often lonelier and less complicated. The key to this situation is the full adjustment of the kids to the divorce, not when the parent is ready.

Once the divorce emotions have been fully dealt with, there is one further hurdle to overcome. A person needs to have the self-confidence to re-enter the dating game. After many years out of the single life, most people have forgotten how the process works and fear it because of this lack of knowledge. Times will have changed and the predominant feeling is one of being "out of it." However, once a person feels ready, there is no easy way to begin. The situation is not unlike going swimming when the water is on the cool side. The best approach is to jump right in. In this case, there is no way to ease into it. Either a date is accepted when one is offered or the nerve has to be found to ask an attractive person out. It often takes courage the first few times, but it will not take long to get back into the swing of it. Times will not have changed that much.

Where To Look

The primary way of meeting new people in your single days was at parties and in the bars. These methods are not really available to mature people for several reasons. First of all, there are no parties with large numbers of single people, as most of your friends are now married and have little in common with singles anymore. The bar scene is geared to young people and tends to feature loud music and crowded dance floors. Meeting someone at a bar is still a remote possibility, but most will feel that they no longer belong there and are uncomfortable. It is hard to talk to someone over the music, and alcohol-fuelled meetings no longer have any attraction. Bars are generally not for older people.

Two single acquaintances of the author, both in their forties, were on a golf trip and decided to try out the local clubs. After the third bar with raucous music and predominantly twentyish patrons, one of the men turned to a young girl and asked, "Where does your mother hang out?" _____

A much better way for divorced and widowed people to meet other unattached people their age is through recreational activities. Joining clubs and engaging in enjoyable activities involving large numbers of people is definitely better than cruising the bars, with the added bonus that these people share an interest in the activity. This provides a common bond right from the start. The main purpose of the activity should still be recreation and relaxation, but you can't meet people by staying at home, so these activities provide the best of both worlds.

The starting point should be to determine what interests you have or what activities have always interested you, but either your spouse did not share them or you did not have the time to engage in them. Most communities have lists of the clubs and groups that provide recreational, artistic, or educational opportunities. Many even publish periodic booklets of these activities. Once you decide what you might like to try, the information is readily available. If you have no idea where to start, pick up one of the city or town publications and peruse the many activities that are listed. While these mostly consist of courses, there will be a wide variety of ideas that may lead to further research and discovery.

Volunteering can provide a meeting place for people of common interests. Again, there will be a community resource list of places that may need volunteers, such as the local hospital, a senior citizen's home, or a food bank. The satisfaction gained from volunteer activities cannot be underestimated, a huge added benefit if the main aim is to meet other unattached people.

One of the new forms of meeting people is speed-dating. This unique concept apparently originated in a Jewish Torah class in Los Angeles in the early nineties. Much parodied in sitcoms, speed-dating usually consists of seven-minute interviews with 10 or 12 different people, following which you decide if you want to pursue a full-fledged date at some other time. While it is often made fun of, it can be worth trying as it brings single people interested in dating together in one location. The process is much faster than going to meetings or classes and trying to get to know someone there, but has the disadvantage of getting very little accurate information in the seven-minute time frame (people can say anything to get your attention). It might involve a few unfortunate dates, but if you are a relatively outgoing person it definitely has its merits.

Another new form of meeting people has become so popular that it requires a section of its own.

Online Dating

If proof were required that the world has changed dramatically, it is found in the virtual explosion of computer use to find a partner. In its infancy in the 1990s, computer dating (or online chatting) was scorned by many who considered it to be reserved for cyber freaks and weirdos. Stories were told with snickers of derision of people who ran off to parts unknown to marry their online correspondent. This is no longer the case. So many people are now using this method of meeting people that the numbers are measured in the tens of millions. Despite the popularity, problems still exist.

The main problem is that the anonymity of sitting behind a computer screen allows a large percentage of users the luxury of exaggerating or minimizing some of their characteristics. A recent article in *Scientific American Mind* magazine found that men tend to falsify their educational level, income, height, age, and *marital status*. This latter characteristic can be the biggest problem; the physical characteristics cannot be hidden once a meeting is arranged, but marital status can be. With women, the main areas of prevarication are weight (a discounting of an average of 19 pounds for ladies in their 40s), physical appearance, and age. Despite these well-known tendencies, the popularity continues to rise. As long as users maintain an open mind about the possibilities of deception, then online dating can be useful, especially for those who either can't find the time to go out or have not got the courage to try a more face-to-face approach.

Another concern about the online dating world is the matchmaking services sold by some of the major profit-oriented organizations. These companies trumpet their "personality tests" that are designed to find the subscriber's perfect match. The problem is that these tests have very little scientific validity and are no better at finding a match than is chatting online with a variety of people. They are also expensive and, since these tests are no more accurate than your own judgment, the cost is not justified.

Because of the above limitations, the usefulness of this dating method

SCOTT WOODING

is limited. It is far better to get out and meet people because of the recreational benefits that come with clubs, classes, and courses. However, for those inhibited by the real world—and that is especially understandable after years out of the dating world and after a bad marital experience—then online dating can certainly be an alternative method of finding a mate. It would seem reasonable that if this is a dating method that you want to try, then you avoid potential embarrassment by not exaggerating your own attributes. Be honest and post only actual photos of yourself. It may not be wise to post your children's pictures on the Net, though, for safety reasons and to avoid upsetting your ex, but it is important to mention that you have them. Honesty is always the best policy if you are serious about dating.

Who to Avoid

While this list could become very long and complicated, the main concern is that you avoid those people who are themselves still married. Since it has already been stated that a basic rule of thumb is that at least a full year after the completion of the divorce process be allowed before starting dating, the same should go for anyone that you might meet. The following categories of potential partners should be avoided at all costs—no matter how attractive they might be:

- Those who are "separated."
- They're "staying together for the kids."
- They "have most things worked out."
- They "can't afford to live separately at this time."
- Those whose divorce is "in the hands of the lawyers."
- They're "just living like brother and sister."

All of these categories are just euphemisms for the fact that the person is still married. Like you, they will.need the time to find out who they have become. There will be too much baggage for most of these people until they have sorted out the same things that you had to. Avoid them like the plague, no matter how nice they appear to be.

What About the Kids

One of the big mistakes that single parents make is to involve their children in their dating experiences too soon. While it is important to let them know that you are considering dating again and equally vital that parents let their kids know when they are going out with someone, there are many steps that need to happen before the kids actually meet and interact with a dating partner. The first step is to sit down with the kids when dating is imminent and to discuss their feelings about the situation. The kids need to know that, for the present, it is just dating, and that you will always let them know if it becomes serious. They also need to understand that no one will ever replace their biological parent. This is a critical step that must not be overlooked.

Beginning dating marks the end of the great dream of a majority of children of divorces—that their parents will get back together again. While they may understand that their parents are lonely and long for companionship, the children still may not want to contemplate the concept that the marriage will never again be an entity. This means that clear and frequent communication with the children is necessary to get their fears and concerns out in the open and to reassure them when necessary.

CHILDREN'S EMOTIONS WHEN THE PARENT STARTS DATING

Fear:
a) That to accept a new person is a betrayal of their other biological parent. Are they being disloyal to this parent and will the parent be upset with them for appearing to tolerate one

SCOTT WOODING

parent's dating?

b) That this new person might replace them as their parent's friend and confidant, or replace them as number one in the parent's heart.

c) That their parent might get hurt again just as he or she was by the divorce.

Excitement: Many have unrealistic expectations about what a new relationship may bring, such as a bigger house, presents, or perhaps just happiness for their parent. _____

This also means that there should be no sneaking around to avoid upsetting them. Kids always figure out where their parent is going and will often leap to the wrong conclusions if they do not have accurate information. In other words, they may assume the relationship is more serious than it actually is. Clear communication and information are necessary—but not in great detail. Definitely you should address the children's fears about replacing their biological parent, about you (and them) possibly getting hurt again if it doesn't work out (many teens really do worry about this aspect of their parent dating), and about letting them know if a relationship becomes serious.

After the fact that you are about to begin dating again is communicated, it is important that the children are not involved in the details of your casual dates. Not only is it important not to say much, it is vital that the children do not meet and socialize with casual dates. This can be a strong temptation if, for example, the date's children are the same age as your own. Wouldn't it be nice if the children could all be friends? Maybe we should take our kids out together? Resist this temptation. Even if the relationship is starting to become serious, do not involve the children yet. Wait until there is a definite chance of remarriage before any social interaction is allowed to occur.

While this may seem drastic, it will be far easier on the children if, when a relationship ends, they have not been involved. While most children will initially resent any newcomer to a relationship, some, due to their own needs and insecurities, will actually bond with the dating partner, only to have him or her disappear when the relationship ends. This will increase those insecurities and create more problems for both the parent and child in the future. For example, after being burned in this way once or twice, many children will avoid an emotional commitment with your future dating partners. This could become a serious problem when Mr. or Ms. Right finally does come along.

In a similar vein, it is important that parents not share details of their sexual life with their children, or worse, have sleepovers with their dating partner. Children do not even want to think of their married parents having sex, much less realize that their single parent is. Teens especially have a strong sense of morality that parents need to respect. There is nothing wrong with having sex with a dating partner if it feels right, but this information should not be conveyed to the children. If sex does happen, make sure it is not in either home—that's what motels are for—and that no mention of it is made to the kids. The main danger is that, if the relationship becomes serious, the children's resentment about the sexual activity will colour their opinion of the new partner. It is usually extremely difficult to introduce a new person to a family. There is no need to make it even harder.

Lori's parents had been divorced for several years and the pleasant, outgoing 14-year-old had become used to a close relationship with her mother. However, she suddenly started seeing the school counsellor on a regular basis. While she babbled happily about her social life and her classes, Lori never seemed to be able to articulate what was bothering her. Finally, after several sessions and some prompting, she blurted out, "My mother is a slut." Knowing how close their relationship had been, the counsellor found this a startling statement. It turned out that Lori's mother had become intimate with her latest boyfriend and decided to tell her daughter the details. Not only did Lori learn that her mother was sleeping with her boyfriend, she heard details that she simply did not want to hear.

When informed, the mother was stunned at Lori's reaction to her revelations. She had developed the type of relationship described earlier, where she leaned on her daughter for emotional support. She also had the idea that honesty was the best policy and so had shared the full details of her sex life. While her intentions were good, Lori's mother did not understand teenage morality, and not only made it impossible for her daughter ever to like her boyfriend, but also strained her own relationship with her daughter. This was a lesson learned the hard way.

Children should be clearly informed that their parent is dating and be allowed to share their concerns and fears about this situation, but details about the person and the relationship should not be shared until the relationship becomes serious. There should be as little social interaction between the kids and the new friend as possible to avoid hurting the children. They have already had one hard emotional shock with the divorce. They don't need any more.

Don't Forget the Ex-Spouse

Most divorced parents who are contemplating dating would see no reason for informing the former spouse of this fact. After all, it is no longer any of his or her business. However, a potential minefield can be avoided by letting the ex know that you are about to resume a social life. Strangely, they still care and are very likely to have an emotional reaction to this fact. This is true even when they have initiated the divorce. Letting them know your plans will have two benefits.

The first is that the ex may be more cooperative if you have the consideration to inform him or her that you want to date again. In other words, this communication may help to keep the interaction required of ex-partners when dealing with the children flowing smoothly. Once again, the power of emotions will become evident if you keep this information to yourself—or worse, if the ex finds out through the kids. For some reason, this latter situation drives former spouses to distraction. They hate this happening even though, deep down, they know it's none of their business. This is also particularly true if the spouse has never resolved the breakup baggage and still harbours guilt/anger emotions. Suddenly, cooperation and flexibility may not be there when you want it, just because the ex has been blindsided by the dating information.

The second benefit to informing ex's is that it will provide a chance to reassure them that nothing will change with regard to the custody arrangements and that you will not be seeking to have the new person replace the biological parent in the children's lives. Once again, this may seem unnecessary, but this step should not be ignored. Divorce is a highly emotional event and emotions surrounding it do not necessarily make sense. All possible precautions should be taken to avoid upsetting the delicate balance that may have taken months to achieve.

Meeting Mr./Ms. Right

With work schedules and the demands of parenting making it difficult to find the time and energy to date, it might take a while to find someone to fall in love with, but the chances are that it will happen eventually. This is especially true if you have been following the advice above and actively looking. Once it starts to happen, it is vital that the process not move too quickly. This is because the situation is not the same as it was back in your single days. Now there are two factors that are different from your original romance. The first is that you have already had one failure and, after experiencing the emotional roller coaster of divorce, you don't want it to happen again. The second is that you may have children to consider. They, too, have experienced the gamut of negative emotions, and it would be cruel and dangerous to put them through them again. With these considerations in mind, it is vital to try to keep your brain working effectively and not let the powerful feelings of love overwhelm it. Some reality checks are in order.

The main one should be to ensure that you are in love for the right reasons. In many cases, the feelings are actually resulting from having the needs created by the divorce filled. These needs include feelings of loneliness, financial pressures, and the desire to ease your parenting pressures by finding a mother or father for the children. It is amazing how these desires can underlie what appears to be real love and can result in your missing some negative qualities in the loved one. It will be difficult, but it is vital to slow down the desire to remarry in order to carefully examine your motives.

Another reality check would be to try to ensure that the person you are falling in love with is not leaning on the relationship to fill his or her own needs. This may be hard to determine, but it certainly needs to be considered and discussed before any plans to marry take shape. This discussion should include:

- How did you get into your first marriages?
- What attracted you to your first mates?
- What went wrong with these marriages?
- What have you learned from your first failures?
- How can you avoid similar mistakes in this new relationship?

This makes for a heavy discussion, but it's a vital one. Things are just not the same as they would have been in a first marriage. If these areas are not covered, the chance of making another mistake is very high. The hard fact is that most people who are contemplating remarriage just do not go through this communication exercise. No wonder the failure rate on second marriages is so high. It is crucial that the former relationships are discussed and the motives for thinking about remarriage examined carefully. It is a whole new situation now and you are, you hope, an older and wiser person. Falling in love with someone cannot be left to brain chemistry and hormones alone. Reason and logic also have to have a place in developing the new relationship.

Involving Your Children

Once a relationship has become serious to the point that remarriage is being seriously contemplated, then, and only then, should the kids be involved. Certainly you have been communicating with them about the fact that you are dating, and you have given them some basic facts about the person, but to this point, the kids should not have met this person. Once you think you've found a keeper, it's time to let your children into the relationship. Now you can go out for dinner together, go to the zoo as a group, or take in the occasional movie. However—*do not expect the kids to like this person!*

This may happen in some circumstances but it is not the general rule—at least not at first. Remember the emotions that children go through when their parents start dating. Fear is the main one. They don't know what is going to happen in the future, especially when it comes to their relationship with the other biological parent. This uncertainty makes most kids leery. They don't want to like this person too much. What if their real dad gets upset? What if this new guy hurts Mom again? What if Dad likes her more than me? All these questions run through the kids' minds and interfere with their ability to like their parent's new friend instantly. Liking and respecting the new person will take time and effort on the part of the parent, in terms of clear and frequent communication about plans and feelings, and on the part of the new love interest.

This means that parents should expect, at the minimum, a very cool reception for the new person. At worst, there might be actual acts of sabotage committed, especially if the children are teenagers. These could include rudeness or refusal to participate in activities. While this may be embarrassing if not expected, these behaviours can often be avoided through the good communication practices described above. Even if they do occur, anger or consequences for the behaviour will not help. Instead, after the date is over and you are back at the home, it is time to reopen the communication channels—calmly—and get the feelings out in the open. A sample dialogue would go something like this:

Mom: *"Wow, you guys really gave Jim a hard time today. Didn't you like him?"*

Kid #1: *"It's not that—he was all right, I guess. I just felt weird."*

Mom: *"What do you mean by weird?"*

Kid #1: *"I thought he was a phoney. Always being nice to us. It's like he was sucking up or something."*

Kid #2: *"I just hated the way he was always touching you. It seemed like it should be Dad doing that. It's hard to get used to."*

Mom: *"Maybe he felt weird, too."*

Kid #1: *"Why would he feel weird?"*

Mom: *"Well, maybe he was afraid you wouldn't like him. He might have been so nice because since he loves me, he wants you to like him, too, but he isn't sure how to do that. Can you guys give him a chance for a while and see if he is actually as nice as I think he is?"*

Kid #2: *"We'll try—but it's really hard."*

Mom: *"I know it is. It's a little strange for me, too. But I think he's a great guy and if you give him some time, I'm sure you kids will see that, too."*

The idea is to allow the children to express their feelings safely. It will not help for the parent to deny these feelings with a statement like, "How can you feel like that—you don't even know him?" That will cut off communication and almost guarantee a repeat performance of their negative behaviour the next time. Instead, allow them to express these feelings and, rather than simply verbally defending the new person, try to give him or her time to win their affection. How much time this will take will depend on the circumstances, but six months to a year is more likely than a few weeks. This is a strange and emotion-laden experience for the children and they need time to adjust to it. Patience and good communication is the answer.

If They're Not Your Kids

If you are seriously dating a person with children, you have a special challenge. You will have to find ways to overcome their initial resistance and to form a bond with them. This is not easy, but is entirely possible if you are patient and persistent. The first step is to realize that his or her children will almost certainly harbour negative feelings toward you. The kids will usually be chagrined to realize that their parent is contemplating remarriage, since that signals the end to any chance that their biological parents will ever get back together. They will see you as an unworthy replacement for their real parent and will therefore resent your relationship with their mom or dad.

Unfortunately, most prospective stepparents don't see this hurdle coming. The great majority of suitors to people with children just don't realize that this resistance will exist and so, when they encounter it, are resentful. The result is that they start to believe that the children are rude or undisciplined and just need their parent to get control of them. This attitude, while definitely the most common one, will be disastrous. Instead of taking months to overcome the initial resistance and develop a relationship, it might now take years—if it happens at all. The resentment of your loved one's children must be expected and considered to be normal and natural. It is the main obstacle to a successful remarriage.

After realizing that there will normally be resistance to your liaison, the next move should be to take steps to slowly and gently overcome this resistance. It is vital to recognize that the process of winning over the children will take time, and not to be discouraged if there is no immediate progress. The emotions that you are trying to work through are deep and strong. They include a biological bond with the estranged parent. If the parent that you are dating has worked through the breakup baggage with his or her children, has taken a long break before dating again, and has thoroughly prepared the kids for meeting you, then the process will not be as difficult. However, most people will not have done this. The task will therefore be a major one and should be considered as important as the relationship with their parent. Ideally, the two of you should work together on this "project" since it is so vital to the success of the relationship.

These are several approaches to bonding with the children of your loved one. The first is to get to know as much about them as possible. This involves their interests, their schoolwork and their friends, and should be accomplished mainly by talking with the children. Whenever you find yourself alone with one of the kids, no matter how briefly, you can ask questions to find their likes and dislikes:

- What grade are they in?
- What's their favourite subject?
- How do they like their teacher(s)?
- What do they like to do for fun outside school and who do they do it with?

These may seem like very simple and basic questions, but they serve two purposes. They help to relax the child or children because you are showing an interest in them and getting them to talk about themselves (everybody's favourite topic). They also give you a wealth of information to build on. If, for example, the child reveals that he takes guitar lessons, then the next time you can ask how the lessons are going and what tunes he is currently playing. Perhaps you could even get him to play something for you.

To do this, you have to remember what you have been told so that you can bring up the topic the next time you see the child. Take notes (afterwards) if you have to, but do not forget what you have been told. If you have to ask the same questions over and over, the child assumes you haven't been listening and you lose points.

Another key step in the bonding process is to make sure the first few times you meet the children involve activities and not just sitting around together watching a movie. Find activities that the kids will enjoy and keep them active. You can still ask your questions and talk to them in quiet moments, but doing fun things is a good way to break the ice with them. This does not mean exotic activities, like a trip to Disneyland, but things like trips to the local leisure centre to swim, excursions to the local zoo, or any other enjoyable pursuits that you can all take part in. This is particularly important if the children are widely different in age as, for example, very young children might not want to take in a baseball game as it is too sedentary and boring for them.

One note of caution is that prospective stepparents need to be careful not to impose their own agendas on the kids. That means that it is important to make the choice of activities a participatory one and not simply one that you want to do. This is not about you; it's about getting to know the children and allowing them to get to know you. It is certainly possible to make suggestions, but try to let the kids have a say in picking the activity or there is a risk of boring them. This will make them irritable and whiny, which often results in anger and frustration in return. Everyone should be having fun, and when the enjoyment begins to wane, it's time to go home.

A second caution is also required. A common tendency early in the relationship with the children is to try too hard to please them. One way of doing this is by constantly bringing them presents. While this might be well-intentioned, it amounts to buying the children's affection—and it won't work. The expectation becomes that every time you come there will be presents, and when this becomes unsustainable, the kids tend to become resentful. Unless it is a birthday or other very special occasion, avoid the temptation to buy them things.

Similarly, always doing what the kids want to do, no matter the cost or the effort required, is also not the answer. The whole process of getting to know the children and developing a relationship with them must be a reasonable one. The focus is on the children, but not to the extent of spoiling them. If their idea is impractical, it is realistic to gently reject it by explaining why it can't work and then replace the idea with some suggestions of your own. The kids can't run the show, but their input is important and should be considered whenever possible.

When You Both Have Kids

If you also have children of your own, then some pre-blending of the families is necessary. Both of the dating partners must now follow the communication steps outlined above to keep their children informed of the progress of the relationship. Then, once it is determined that the relationship might have a future, the next action is to meet the partner's children individually—without the children meeting each other. Blending families is extremely difficult and cannot be rushed. Some parents, for example, think that it will be great for the kids to have new friends and assume that just because they are similar in ages they will automatically be friends. That would be nice, but it almost never happens like that. While the full details of the special issues involved in blending families will be discussed in Chapter 5, suffice it to say that when both partners have children of their own, the dating process must be even slower than for potential stepparents who do not have children.

If all goes well, with each parent establishing a relationship with their new partner's children, a process that could take several months, then the children can meet. Once again, it should be at a fun activity, but now the complexity of the blending process can start to be seen. Trying to find an activity that everyone can enjoy just got far more complicated. Both of the parents need to work on this task. With some persistence, such an activity can usually be found. Awkwardness and even some hostility between the children must be expected. While the parents have known each other for some time and are in love, that has nothing to do with the children. They are strangers to each other and, in some ways, rivals. With tremendous luck, the kids will all like each other, but this will not be the norm. The first activity should be structured so that everyone can have fun and so that as little communication between the kids as possible is required. In other words, they should not be left alone together any more than necessary.

Every outing from this point need not include all the children, but some of them should. Each blended activity should be followed by a communication session held by each parent for his or her own children. This is something that is rarely done but that can pay huge dividends. The idea is to get the kids talking about how the day went and how things are going with the other dating partner's children. Once again, be mainly in listening mode. If the children have concerns, don't try to defend the issue, just ask why they feel this way. A sample conversation could go something like this:

Julie: "I hate Eric. He's a real jerk."

Mom: "Wow! That's a strong feeling. Why do you feel this way?"

Julie: "Today he wouldn't let me play with his video game."

Mom: "Did he do anything else?"

Julie: "No—but he kept playing with the game and wouldn't talk to me."

Mom: "That does sound a bit antisocial, but did you consider that maybe he might be a bit shy? After all, he doesn't really know you."

Julie:	"Well, maybe. But he could at least try being nice to me."
Mom:	"Let's give him some time. I'm sure things will be better once you get to know each other."

Once again, the idea is to get the feelings out without denying them, and then plant an idea that may help later. Without good communication, conflicts could simmer undetected, then flare up as a serious matter after the marriage. If a major concern emerges, such as a serious personality clash between two of the children, then it may be necessary to discuss the issue with your partner and try to find a solution from both ends. The kids don't have to all be friends, but you certainly don't want any of them to be enemies.

If it seems like almost every section of this chapter is recommending that the dating process proceed very slowly, your perception is accurate. There should be years between a divorce and a remarriage. While that may seem to be a very conservative approach, when children are involved, it is impossible to be too careful. Every move needs to be considered and often communicated. While loneliness and love are powerful forces, it is vital that time be given to allow the brain to function. The remarriage failure rate is far too high, and this is mainly because the process was rushed and not carefully thought out. If done slowly and carefully, the chances of a successful second marriage should be very high.

Remarriage

If all has gone well in the dating process and love has resulted, the next logical step is to contemplate a more permanent relationship. While this is always a serious step, when children from a previous relationship are involved, it is even more serious. Careful preparation and good planning become essential components to the success of second marriages involving children; such a relationship is much more complicated than either first marriages or remarriages without any children. While this statement seems like common sense, it is amazing how the power of love can override caution and cause otherwise sensible people to race to the altar totally unprepared for the challenges that await. The focus of this chapter is to identify the potential hazards to a successful remarriage when stepchildren are involved so that they do not suddenly appear and jeopardize the relationship.

Why Not Just Live Together?

In past generations, making a relationship more permanent clearly meant marriage, but times have changed and many couples now first think about moving in together without marrying. Normally cohabitation, or living together, is a step taken to see if a couple is compatible. This has become acceptable in modern society and no longer has any stigma attached to it. However, the situation is different when children are involved.

Few social scientists would disagree that children need a stable home setting to develop self-confidence and emotional stability. The research is also clear that divorce can have serious emotional consequences for the majority of children. In order for them to recover from these effects, it is even more important that children of divorce find stability in future domestic settings. This stability is much more difficult to achieve when their parents are cohabiting instead of being married.

The message that cohabitation gives to children is that their parent's relationship may not be permanent since there has been no long-term commitment made. This is generally an accurate perception because living together is normally for the purpose of testing the marital waters. So long as their parent and the parent's love interest are not married, there is much less stability to the home situation. Naturally, the longer this relationship lasts, the more stable the situation becomes, but it is never the same as marriage. This requires a long-term commitment that children of most ages clearly understand. Without this commitment, the children are given the message that, while the adults may love each other, they may not always be together. For children who have already been through one disastrous relationship, this provides just enough of an element of doubt to prevent them from relaxing and feeling safe and comfortable in their new home situation.

For parents who are contemplating a domestic relationship with their love interest, marriage is the only situation in which their children will feel safe and comfortable. If you are not sure that you want to marry again, then continued dating is the answer. Cohabitation may be fine for those who have never been married or who do not have children, but it is too uncertain for most children, especially those who have already been through the emotional turmoil of a divorce.

SCOTT WOODING

Pre-Marriage Planning

Planning is necessary for any wedding, whether first, second, or other. For a first marriage, all that is usually necessary is having a place to live and deciding on details of the ceremony. The latter has traditionally been the bride's domain, but recent social trends have tended to include the groom as well. For a second marriage where children are involved, the future success of the new relationship can be considerably improved by extending the premarital planning much further. In this case, there is no question that both parties need to be intimately involved. The planning required falls into several key areas.

Financial

Money problems are a major cause of a large percentage of marriage failures, and second marriages are no exception. However, there are several added complications in remarriages. The first is that there is more financial history involved in these relationships. As in all marriages, the partners have their personal fiscal history from their birth family, such as whether they were raised in a wealthy family that spent money freely or in a poorer family that watched every penny. In addition, they also have the financial patterns of their first marriages to consider. Their partner may have been very tight with his or her money, leading to considerable friction between them. On the other hand, the spouse may have been a complete spendthrift whose lack of money-management skills kept them constantly in debt. Finally, the prospective partners may have developed certain habits during the time period after their previous marriages, when they were single and not subject to the controls or lack of controls of a relationship. This newfound financial independence may be very difficult to give up in the new relationship, leading to serious friction if compromises are not reached. The case of John and Angela clearly indicates how complex the situation can be.

Angela was an only child who had been raised by relatively wealthy and indulgent parents. As a child, she never lacked for money and was given most of the things she wanted. Her first marriage had been a disaster for several reasons, but her spending habits had been a major factor in the friction between them. Despite a limited budget (her first husband was a firefighter and she was a stay-at-home mom to their two children), she purchased furniture, clothing, and gifts whenever she felt the need. As a result, their credit cards were constantly at maximum and her husband was at his wit's end as to how to get out of debt. His money-management skills were actually very good, but Angela was constantly angry with him for being such a "Scrooge." The relationship lasted for nine years before the constant discord, mostly from their financial problems, ended it.

Despite being a full-time mother for several years, Angela had a good education and was able to find a very good job after her divorce. Her parents financed the purchase of her home, so Angela once again found herself able to spend at will. All was well until she met John, a teacher who had been divorced for two years and who had two children of his own. Very soon after they married, the financial problems started again. While both were working and money shouldn't have been a problem, Angela's out-of-control spending habits again began to take their toll. They had never actually discussed finances before their marriage, and it was just assumed that John, being the responsible male, would pay the household expenses. Angela then felt free to spend her salary as she wished. This left John in a constant state of financial difficulty, making it hard for him to afford his child-support payments and almost impossible for him to pay for some of the school field trips and extra expenses that so often arise with children.

The result was that John's ex-wife was constantly harassing him for money. This prolonged the break-up baggage indefinitely and resulted in considerable stress for John and pressure on the new marriage. Since he and Angela had never discussed finances before the marriage, they were well into the problem before it was recognized. After years of unlimited spending, Angela had no sense of fiscal restraint, and suddenly her second marriage was also in trouble.

Spending habits of the past can haunt a new marriage if finances aren't carefully planned well before the couple moves in together. This is especially true since there are so many more variables to consider in a second marriage. For example, as in the case above, there are expenses involved with children, no matter which parent they are living with. These have to be taken into account. There may be property from the previous relationship. For example, if one of the partners already owns a home, who pays the mortgage? What about support payments to the ex? While it may be impossible to plan for all the contingencies, most of them can be determined if time and effort are spent on this subject.

The first place to start is with bank accounts and personal allowances. Each partner should have a personal bank account, along with one joint family account into which a set amount of money from each person is transferred each month. The joint account is for bill payments and other common expenses. Before the marriage, the partners need to sit down and list all their bills and expected monthly commitments. These will normally consist of mortgage payments, utility bills, telephones, vehicle payments, and commuting expenses. Anything that both partners and their children share in should be paid for from this joint account. Then, the amount that each will contribute to this bill-paying account should be determined. Naturally, this amount may have to be revisited in the future, but for the present, it can be set reasonably accurately, and a monthly transfer arrangement can be made with the bank that will take the thinking out of this process.

Which partner is to pay these bills should also be decided at this time, along with the actual bill-paying mechanics. Fixed monthly payments can be withdrawn automatically and utility and telephone bills can all be paid on the Internet. This reduces time and effort, although it can still be a frustrating process to oversee the regular monthly drain on the income. The partner who is the most patient and who is more methodical should take on this responsibility.

Many couples adopt a system that has each paying specific bills from their own accounts. This can work, too, but a single-payment account system is usually more effective. There is also a trust factor involved in having a joint family account, and while this may seem like a tiny factor in the relationship, every little bit counts. Payments that are unique to each spouse, such as child-support payments or college accounts for kids from the first marriage, should probably come from the individual accounts if each partner is working. If it is decided that one parent will stay home with the kids, then all payments should come from the joint account. They just need to be identified and possibly negotiated ahead of time.

In conjunction with these decisions, the next step is to set savings goals for retirement or future major expenditures. This might best be done with the help of a financial counsellor, for two reasons. These trained people know far more about the various savings vehicles and tax-savings methods than most laymen. This allows for more choices than just a straight savings account. Also, a financial counsellor provides a buffer in what can often be a rather emotional situation. Unless there is plenty for everyone, which is not a normal scenario, issues around money are almost always emotional. A neutral person can be knowledgeable enough to keep the situation under restraint so that the most effective decisions for the future can be made.

Darryl and Susan were definitely an odd couple. He had a PhD in biology and owned his own successful company, while she worked as a clerk in a local food market. He had been married before and had two children from that relationship, while she, at thirty-two, had never been married. Despite these differences, their relationship had lasted for seven years and marriage was finally being planned. Unfortunately, the relationship hit a major snag just before the wedding and counselling was needed to repair the damage.

The problem was money. It had taken seven years to get to the marriage because of their frequent arguments over this topic. Susan constantly overspent her salary, was continually late paying her bills, and usually failed to file her tax returns on time. Darryl, being a methodical scientist, was exactly the opposite and could not understand what her problem was. He even tried to get her to do their household bills to teach her about money, but a few weeks after giving her the job, he found all the invoices on the floor of her car. He was furious and another huge argument ensued.

What Darryl did not realize was that Susan had two major problems that prevented her from being good with money matters. The first was her learning style. While Darryl was a concrete thinker whose mind ran in a very logical pattern, Susan was an abstract, random person who had great difficulty thinking in a sequential manner. She was more artistic and creative than Darryl was, but had great difficulty with structure and sequence. This was not caused by a lack of intelligence but strictly by their very different thinking or learning styles. As a result, accounting of any kind was difficult for her.

Added to this problem was that Susan had a learning disability. While she could read well, she could not put things down on paper effectively. Writing and spelling were very hard for her, making the filling out of any forms a huge chore. This made bill-paying and tax-filing a painful job that she avoided at all costs. Darryl had no such problem.

The result was that until Darryl realized how difficult it was for Susan to do anything with money, they fought constantly. It took the counsellor to point out their differences and suggest that Darryl handle the finances and set up their accounts so that Susan could not overspend at will. Susan had not realized why she hated financial matters either, and her understanding of the problem also led her to work harder at being more fiscally responsible. If these differences had been recognized and dealt with earlier in the rela-tionship, instead of each being angry with the other for their intol-erance, the marriage could have happened much sooner.

As the case above illustrates, understanding each other's financial capa-bilities is vital to a sound relationship. Each partner needs to understand his or her own capabilities and limitations, and the subject needs to be thor-oughly analyzed before marriage. Unfortunately, this is rarely done, but it certainly needs to be before the next step is attempted. This is the setting of personal spending limits—the discretionary money that each partner can spend every week or month, without consulting the other. The difficult part is in setting this limit. If each partner has an income, then this amount can easily be just what is left over after the bills and the savings have been deducted. If one partner does not have an income, then an allowance amount needs to be set and transferred regularly into the other's account.

It is this discretionary amount that often creates the problems, as past spending habits come into play here. Setting the amount might be difficult enough, but sticking to it is even harder for some people. For those with freer spending histories, it might be necessary to ensure that the personal account does not have overdraft protection, but this really isn't the answer. Self-discipline is vital in a marriage when it comes to finances, and it is immature and unfair that a partner can do all this planning only to have it thrown to the winds on a regular basis. If a partner can't curb spending, then counselling may be necessary to solve this problem quickly before it becomes a major obstacle to a happy marriage.

The above advice must seem like common sense to many people, but it is amazing how often this planning process is not followed, resulting in everything from frequent bickering to the total dissolution of the marriage. Careful financial planning has to occur before the marriage, and it has to be modified, or at least reviewed, yearly, at a minimum. Once set, adjust-ments are simple to make, but this process should not be ignored in the romantic belief that love conquers all.

Housing

Every newly married couple needs a place to live, but remarriages where children are involved take extra planning and consideration. If one partner already owns a home, it may seem logical to live there; if both partners have their own places, then it would seem that a decision would need to be made between these two residences. Such factors as house value and size of payments must naturally be taken into account, but there is more to deciding where to live than the financial aspects or the convenience of a residence that is already owned.

One major concern should be location. If at all possible, the children should not be moved out of their home neighbourhood. This is particularly true if the children are teenagers. Their friends are of paramount importance at this age, and moves are very difficult for them, especially if one or more is shy or of a quieter nature and friends are not easily made. If two families are blending, then at least one of the families will have to move, and it might be easier for the family with the younger children to change residences.

Another consideration is the location of the other biological parent or parents. The closer the residences, the better. Again, this is extremely important for teenagers, who might not want an extended absence from their friends in order to see their other parent. As well, a greater distance between residences means more time and more organization needed to get the kids back and forth. The location of the residence is an important decision that should be discussed thoroughly, not only between the marital partners but with the children as well.

HOUSING HINT

Whenever possible involve the children in the decision making right from the start. If you are buying a new house, get the kids' opinion first. If there is a decision to make about rooms, let the children have their input. While this may seem like letting the inmates run the asylum, it helps to make them feel better about a potential move by allowing them some responsibility. You will be surprised at their maturity and decision-making ability and, when they have input, the kids tend to respect the final decision more.

This does not mean that you have to abide by their decisions. There may be some practical considerations that the children do not understand. In this case it is important to explain to the youngsters why you can't do as they suggest. Children appreciate this candour and the fact that you have at least listened to them, and this makes a difficult situation much more comfortable for everyone. _____

A second residential consideration should be where the children will sleep. Bedrooms are extremely important to children, and allocation of rooms for them should not be done haphazardly. If possible, each child should have his or her own room. If this is impossible, then careful thought should be put into which children will have to double up. This is easier for young children, but if families are blending, then the situation can become complicated. It is always a good principle to involve the children themselves in these decisions, even the young ones. While you may not be able to leave all the decisions to them, kids usually take this kind of responsibility seriously so that their input can be very useful.

A similar concern would be where to house children who live with their other parent when they come for weekends or visitations. This is critical for teenagers, who need more privacy than younger children, but all youngsters need to feel at home in their non-custodial parent's residence. Cramming them in with their siblings, or worse, with their stepsiblings, can cause the children not to want to visit as often, if at all. The presence of a stepparent may already have made the situation awkward, so creating a physical environment as attractive as possible needs to be a priority so

· SCOTT WOODING

that the children are comfortable in the non-custodial setting.

Finally, there are some emotional factors that, as impractical as they may be, can be of concern. For example, there are the memories and the comfort levels that the children might associate with their original residence. If the divorce was a particularly angry one, they might not want to stay in the same house; on the other hand, if the break-up was relatively amicable, the kids might prefer to stay where they already feel at home.

Another emotional concern might be associations that a new spouse may make with the residence that was once inhabited by the new partner's ex. For some, this can be very inhibiting and, for more practical people, hard to understand. It would be unwise to completely ignore these feelings just because they are not logical. Home should be a safe and comfortable place for everyone, and if strong emotions interfere with this comfort level, then they need to be resolved.

For many reasons, then, it is vital that the housing issue be thoroughly discussed both with the prospective marital partners and with the children involved. This will be much more than just a house; it will be everyone's home.

TODD'S ROOM

Todd was just five when his mother, Jennifer, remarried. John had never been married before, came from a stern disciplinary family, and was himself a law-enforcement officer. After three years of marriage, the couple had a daughter, followed two years later by another daughter. John was a good parent to his own children but struggled to connect with Todd, who suffered from attention deficit hyperactivity disorder (ADHD) and was, therefore, often difficult to control. John's methods involved strict rules and very firm consequences that often brought him in conflict with Jennifer, who took a more understanding approach.

The conflict over the parenting of Todd came to a head just after the second daughter was born. The couple lived in a three-bedroom house, and so each daughter was given one of the existing rooms and a room for Todd was built in the basement. After several months, Todd began complaining that he did not like the relative isolation of the basement—he wanted a room on the main floor where he could be closer to the family. John viewed this as weakness and childishness and refused to budge on the issue. The result was building tension between Jennifer and John that finally came to a head after Todd had been in the basement for two years. The marriage began to go downhill and even with counselling it could not be saved. What started as a housing issue became the showcase issue in this troubled marriage, as it clearly seemed that the stepchild was being discriminated against over the natural children. ————————

The Kids

Premarital planning for remarriages must take into account several different concerns with regard to the children if the marriage is to get off on the right foot. Certain assumptions are often made before the marriage and are not dealt with until problems appear. One such is that the spouse to whom the children belong will be responsible for everything related to them, including driving them places, making their lunches, supervising their homework and, above all, disciplining them. This assumption is usually far too wide-ranging as, on many occasions, some help in these areas would not only be appreciated but might be necessary.

Another assumption is that the new family will do everything together and, while this goal is admirable, it is not usually practical and is definitely impractical in a blended family. Sometimes parents need to spend time with their own children, and this need should be respected by the new spouse without resentment. The goal should certainly be to get to the

SCOTT WOODING

point where everyone is just one family, but that usually takes years to accomplish.

Once these assumptions are dispensed with, it is time to make some plans. These should be based on chores related to the children's being shared between the spouses, no matter whose children they are. It may not be necessary to allocate every individual job; it might be enough just to agree to share the load. Some particularly important chores—lunches or driving kids to extracurricular activities—may actually have to be scheduled for particular parents. This schedule might change with each season, so it will have to be revised periodically, but at least the new couple will get into the habit of organizing a schedule.

An area that absolutely must be discussed before the marriage is that of disciplinary philosophies. This is such an important topic that a later chapter will be devoted to it. For now, suffice it to say that it is crucial that the potential spouses realize that although they come from different family backgrounds and had dissimilar experiences in their first marriages, if a common process is not developed for dealing with the disciplinary challenges that children can present, the new marriage might not survive. The topic is that important. While it may take a few experiences to actually determine how the partners will meet these challenges, some initial planning can be done. Rules and responsibilities certainly fall into this category. All children should have some responsibilities around the house and, particularly for older children, there has to be some rules. Both rules and responsibilities should be determined at a family meeting where considerable give and take is allowed. Fairness is an important concept for teenagers and discussions allow them to be heard. This they consider fair. While parents must retain the final say, input from all sources should first be gathered so that as fair a system as possible can develop.

One of the odder but still important aspects of premarital planning with the kids is what they should call the prospective stepparent. Many will already be calling this person by his or her first name, but they may be unsure if this is to be a permanent practice or if they are expected the call the new parent "Mom" or "Dad." This too will require consultation with the children. Ask them what they are comfortable with. In many cases they will start out with the first name and then later start to use "Mom" or "Dad." In other cases, where the biological parent stays closely connected with the children, this may never happen. It doesn't actually matter what word they use, as it is the relationship that is important, but it is vital that they are comfortable. Forcing them to call the stepparent something is a very poor idea and may lead to deterioration of the relationship.

Visitation schedules is another topic that needs prior discussion. These can be highly disruptive to a new family's life and it should not be assumed that the stepparent knows all about them. If the kids will be going to their other parent's place, or visiting this one on a regular basis, the schedule and the possible ramifications of this visitation shuffle need to be clear. This includes transportation to and from the other parent's place, unscheduled changes when something important comes up, housing, and any activities that might have to be planned when the non-custodial kids show up. All this is incredibly disruptive and is not present in a "normal" marriage. Do non-custodial kids who show up every other weekend have to do chores? Who disciplines them when necessary? All these questions and implications need a thorough discussion.

The Ceremony

The bride and her family have traditionally done the planning for the great event in the first marriage, although this has been changing in recent generations. For prospective stepfamilies, it must be a combined planning process.

The first factor to be considered is how much notice the children should be given about the upcoming nuptials. The kids should be informed as soon as the question is popped. All too often, kids find out just before the wedding and don't have time to absorb the coming change and to ask questions about it. This breeds resentment that does not have to be there.

Parts should be found in the ceremony for as many of the children as possible. They will accept the idea much better if they are actually part of the planning and part of the ceremony itself. There are many possible roles for the children to fill. Sometimes creativity will be called for—three flower girls instead of one, for example—but this can be part of the fun. It is important for kids to feel important and valued as members of the new family, and including them in the ceremony is a great way to do this.

Another consideration is the guest list. While the problem of inviting Aunt Mary who has been feuding with Auntie Grizelda would be a concern in any wedding plan, in the case of a remarriage, there are questions about friends from the first marriage and relatives—especially grandparents—of the children's other biological parent. Compromises are definitely necessary. If, for reasons of cost or space, someone who perhaps would normally be there can't be invited, then call to let them know this reason, to avoid hurt feelings and potential future relationship problems.

Usually the ceremonies for remarriages are not as elaborate as those for first marriages, possibly due to a "been there, done that" kind of thinking, but this depends on the happy couple. If one partner—especially the bride—has never been married before, then a big wedding may be desired. The issues can loom very large, and considerable discussion and planning need to go into the ceremony, even if it is not that elaborate. There are many more factors to consider in remarriages than there are for first ones.

Egads! By now prospective stepparents may be second-guessing their decision to marry. But have faith; it's not actually that bad if the time is taken to examine all these novel areas that do not exist for first marriages. Love is a powerful force, but it is just an emotion. It doesn't actually solve anything; it just makes us feel great. Planning is still required to avoid conflict later in the relationship, and this need for preparation is the great difference in stepparenting and blending families. It is definitely not as easy as a first marriage, but it can be just as rewarding if the homework is done.

Readers have probably already noticed how often it has been suggested in this book to involve the children. This may be a new concept for many, but its importance cannot be overstated. The more it is possible to involve children in a remarriage, the more comfortable and valued they feel. The gaining of a stepparent is a frightening process for most young children, and they need to know that they are not going to be relegated to second place in their biological parent's life. Involving them as much as possible is one way to show them that this will not be the case. The idea is not to let them run any of these processes, but it is amazing how mature and insightful they can be when given the chance. Listening to their ideas and opinions can never be a bad idea. If some of these suggestions or thoughts can't be accepted, then the reasons for this should be given. It should not be considered demeaning for them to do this, but instead it should be considered to be a key part of the process when adding a stepparent or two to the family. —————

Remarriage Relationships

When people marry, they expect their spouse to think mainly of them. They prefer to think that they are the most important person in their spouse's life. The primary relationship, then, is with the spouse. When children come along, their needs become very important as well, so that a secondary relationship is formed. However, since both parents have a biological tie to these kids, their own relationship remains paramount, with a common bond to the children.

In second marriages that include children from an earlier liaison, the situation is much more complicated. There are multiple relationships and priorities in these associations that will likely come as a major shock to most unsuspecting brides and grooms. If these relationships are not understood, discussed, and accommodated effectively, then they can actually cause the demise of the new marriage.

To understand the nature and complexity of these relationships, it might be useful to start with a diagram. The simplest situation would be when a man with no children marries a lady with kids from her previous marriage. The relationships are designated by the arrows.

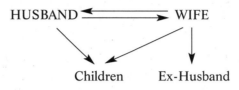

In this particular case, the husband has just two relationships, one with his wife and the other with his stepchildren. His wife would be his major relationship, while his relationship with his stepchildren would be of secondary importance. If all goes well, this latter relationship might become very good, but it would be unlikely ever to become as important as the one with his wife. On the other hand, the wife in this situation has three relationships to maintain. The one with her children is likely to be her major relationship, since she has been raising them for several years before she met her new husband. There may also be some protective factors involved in this relationship that make it even stronger. Mom may feel guilty, or at least concerned, about the effects the divorce had on her children and will be more protective of them as a result. She will be accustomed to putting their needs first and this habit may be hard to break when she remarries. This can be very difficult for the new husband to accept.

The extra relationship for the wife in this case is with her ex-husband. When children are involved, the ex-spouses usually remain involved in their upbringing with visitation rights and everything that implies. This means that the ex-husband is never completely out of his former wife's life. This added relationship could be a complicating factor for the new husband, depending on how harmonious his wife's relationship with her ex actually is. If the relationship is poor, then this will add stress and make their marriage much more difficult.

This means that there are already two major differences between remarriages and first unions that could cause stress between the spouses. In the above case, the new husband has to be emotionally prepared for these differences if the marriage is to succeed. Even more important, the spouses should be working together to make the relationship between them at least as strong as that between the wife and her children. Communication, which is vital to all marriages, then becomes even more important in stepparenting situations, since the chances of conflict as a result of the confusion in the relationships and the stress that can result are so much higher than in a first marriage.

The above relationships diagram would have similar implications if it had been the husband who had the children and an ex-wife. In this case it would be the new wife who would have to deal with the emotional stressors created by the bonds between her husband, his children, and his ex-wife. This is certainly not the idyllic situation that she may have visualized for her marriage. The extra variations on the standard marriage theme may be too difficult for many stepparents to cope with if they are not fully prepared. The problem is that only a small number are prepared, as society has too few mechanisms, in the form of courses or seminars, to explain the extra pressures that often result from stepparenting.

If one spouse with children adds extra relationships, and therefore potential stressors, to a marriage, then the complications that result from both parents having children are obviously multiplied. A look at the relationship diagram will clearly show this.

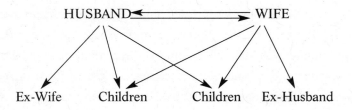

SCOTT WOODING

In this case, each spouse has four relationships to contend with, all at different levels. This hierarchy of relationships will usually be in the following order:

- Relationship with own children.
- Relationship with spouse.
- Relationship with spouse's children.
- Relationship with ex-spouse.

Once again, the aim will be to get the first three of these levels on a more equal basis, with initial focus on raising the relationship with the spouse to the top level. As is often the case, communication is the answer, both with the children and with each other. There has to be a mechanism where perceived or apparent unfairness can be discussed and resolved. After this, the next step will be to raise the level of the relationships with the stepchildren up to the quality of the first two.

Initially, it is important that the protagonists in remarriages understand the variety and nature of these many relationships. Once it is understood that they exist, the spouses must work together at keeping the first three in the hierarchy at an almost even degree. What would be ideal is that the relationship between the spouses comes first on the list, with relationships with all the children, both biological and step, coming a close second. If this can be obtained, then family life will attain an almost Brady Bunch state—a mythical standard, perhaps, but one well worth striving for.

Maintaining a Strong Marriage

Often there are so many challenges to stepparenting and blending families that the last thing that gets attention is the marriage. Developing a relationship with the stepchildren, getting used to new housing, organizing schedules, working, and driving children to their activities all seem to take precedence over the marriage. At first this is not a problem, as the new marriage usually has a momentum of its own. The strong emotional bond that inspired the marriage is initially enough to keep the relationship temporarily solid. However, if no attention is paid to it, then eventually the rigors of daily life may cause the relationship to erode. This is true of any marriage, but remarriages when children are involved have extra challenges that will wear away that bond faster than normal. For this reason some preventative measures are necessary to maintain a strong marriage.

Dates

The first maintenance procedure is the simplest: the marital partners have to have some time alone. A weekly date is one of the easiest and most effective techniques to accomplish this. Many newlyweds will protest that they are too busy to take this time. This is a common concern of most parents in today's fast-paced society. However, since prevention is far easier than a cure, taking the time to spend a few hours each week alone with your new spouse can become an important mechanism for keeping the relationship healthy. It is also an excellent time for communication without the myriad interruptions that occur at home.

These dates don't have to be fancy or expensive. A movie, a dinner at a modestly priced restaurant, or just a couple of hours at the local bar or pub after dinner can all be effective. They also don't have to be routine. One of the techniques for spicing up the weekly date is to take turns planning it. With a little creativity and preparation, each week can bring a new restaurant, a play, or a concert that can add variety and interest to these outings. It is important, though, that the weekly dates involve just the marital couple. Adding friends or relatives to the situation does not allow for the communication that is vital to the preservation of the marriage. Group activities can also be done, of course, but date night should be reserved just for marriage maintenance.

SCOTT WOODING

Family Meetings

Another effective marriage-maintenance technique is to utilize frequent family meetings to solve problems. This highly effective technique is rarely used in most families, yet it is simple to do and takes very little time. It can help preserve the marriage by getting problems aired that could fester and create a wedge between husband and wife. A key example of this would be when children in a blended family feel that their stepparent is treating his or her own kids better than he is treating them. This is an incredibly divisive issue that can create strong resentment in kids, even though it may be unfounded. A vicious cycle starts to occur with the kids resenting the stepparent and showing this anger in various ways. The stepparent then complains to the biological parent that his or her kids are being rude and uncooperative. The biological parent then talks to the kids about improving their behaviour, which only increases the kids' resentment because they feel the stepparent is the problem and not them. The vicious cycle is thus perpetuated and never actually solved. The cycle diagram would be as follows:

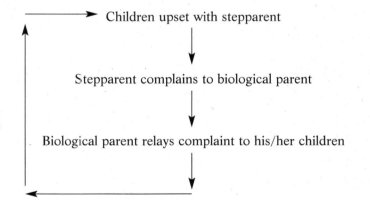

Children upset with stepparent

Stepparent complains to biological parent

Biological parent relays complaint to his/her children

A family meeting could easily solve this issue by allowing the behaviour that caused the concern to be brought up and discussed. In this case there may be substance to the concern, but not always. Stepchildren often expect that biological parents will favour their own children and see supporting evidence that is not actually there. By bringing up these supposed slights and exposing them to the family, they can be explained and interpreted so that all can understand. This technique also helps parents to analyze their own behaviour as they may be doing things to upset their stepchildren without realizing it.

While most adults have attended meetings in their workplace—often ad nauseum—few have conducted them at home. Those held at home are similar, but require some modifications because of the perceived power hierarchy. Meetings in the workplace may be conducted by the boss, but most of the participants are at a relatively equal level in power and maturity. This is not the case at home, where the adults have disproportionate levels of both power and maturity, which can inhibit the children from saying anything. For this reason, some rules need to be established. They can be summarized as follows:

- Hold the meetings on a regular basis, preferably weekly and on the same date and time, so that a routine is established. This is particularly important in the early days of the marriage.
- Rotate the chairmanship. Although there may be some children who are too young, most are capable of being the chairman once the process is understood.
- Allow each person to speak until the point is made. Do not allow interruptions or the meeting will descend into argument and chaos.
- Ensure that everyone gets a chance to speak. Some children are quieter and more inhibited than others, so it's up to the chairman to make sure everyone has an equal chance to share their concerns.
- Keep anger and emotion out of the meeting. This can be one of the biggest challenges, as many issues can be emotionally charged, even for the adults. This, too, is the chairman's job, but initially the adults will have to make certain that a calm and supportive atmosphere is maintained.

SCOTT WOODING

- Keep the meetings as brief as possible as children's attention spans are relatively short.

If these guidelines are followed the meetings will be surprisingly effective. Marriage-testing issues will not be allowed to fester if they can be aired in a safe and supportive environment, and if the issues raised are effectively followed up so that solutions decided on are actually implemented.

Communication

One of the key issues in any marriage is how to communicate emotional issues so that solutions are found and arguments don't occur. For some reason, effective communication techniques are never taught anywhere in our society and yet they are the key to a strong marriage. While this issue is too large to cover completely in this book, knowledge of some basic techniques will facilitate good communication so that serious issues can be resolved and arguments can be avoided.

The first, and most important, communication technique is to focus on not allowing negative emotions to enter a discussion. Anger and defensiveness can instantly block communication and result in heated exchanges. The fact that anger has no place in modern society was discussed in Chapter 1. It only brings the desire to win or hurt. It was never meant to be used in a loving relationship, but it usually seems to happen far too frequently. Anger usually enters a discussion situation when one of the participants is placed on the defensive. Because he or she has no rational explanation for the behaviour, rather than admit being wrong, the person on the defensive attacks. A typical example goes something like this:

He: *"You didn't pay the electrical bill again this month. Now we have to pay interest on it."*

She: *(Immediately on the defensive)* *"It wasn't my fault; you never gave me the bill."*

He:	"It was right there with the other mail. You know it has to be paid every month. Why don't you have some sort of reminder system?"
She:	"Well, you always *forget to put gas in the car. Why don't you have a reminder system for that?*"
He:	(Getting frustrated) "We're not talking about the car. We're talking about the bills."
She:	"You don't have to raise your voice. You always get mad at me. You never *give me credit for what I do.*"
He:	"Well if you would do something once in a while, I would have something to give you credit for."
She:	(Loud and sarcastic) "That's right. I never *do any-thing. I'm just useless around here. Why don't you go find someone who does everything for you?*"

... and the argument continues, involving much yelling and finally the slamming of doors, possibly ending with someone sleeping on the couch. The worst part of such a scenario is that no solution has been found to the problem of the electrical bill. The "discussion" almost instantly descended into an argument that resulted in things being said that were only designed to hurt. The essence of this one was that the wife felt attacked by her husband and almost instantly became defensive. The reason for her initial defensiveness was probably that this issue has arisen before and was not resolved. She then went on the offensive herself, first blaming the husband for the problem, and then attacking his behaviour. Suddenly both people were on the attack, harsh words were said, and hurt feelings were the result.

A secondary issue in communication is the use of certain "trigger" words. These are words that will definitely trigger a defensive reaction. In the above case the words *always* and *never* are not italicized because they fall into this category. Only rarely are these words true. Since there are very few actions that always or never occur, the use of these statements will usually sidetrack the discussion with this new issue, as exemplified by the following:

He: *"You never pay the bills on time!"*

She: *"That's not true. I paid them on time in December. You never give me credit for anything."*

... and the argument continues in a new direction.

The solution first involves learning how to phrase issues so that defensiveness does not occur. In the above case, the problem started right from the husband's first statement. If he had thought about it before venting his frustration, he would have realized that they had argued about this issue before and that pointing out his wife's financial deficiencies was only going to cause another fight. The solution is to utilize an "I" statement instead of attacking the spouse. This technique, originated by Dr. Thomas Gordon, involves stating your feelings about a situation rather using than a "you"-oriented message. The "you" statement is usually a guaranteed way to put the other person on the defensive. A replay of the above argument using an "I" statement would sound something like this:

He: *"I'm worried about our electrical bill situation."*

She: *"Why?*

He: *"Well it didn't get paid again this month and so we have to pay interest on it."*

She: *"Well, I never saw the bill and just didn't think about it."*

He: *"It seems that we need to develop a system so that the bills don't get overlooked. Any ideas?*

She: *"Well, we could put 'Pay bills' on the calendar just before the end of the month as a reminder."*

He: *"Okay. Let's try that and see if it works."*

This discussion started out in a similar way, but because an "I" statement was used, the wife's response was slightly softer. The husband's use of "we" was also an important contribution to keeping the discussion from becoming an attack. The wife's relative lack of emotion in response led to her husband's staying calmer, and a potential solution to the problem was found. This simple but effective technique takes some practice, but saves an amazing amount of wear and tear on a marriage. In the case of a step-parenting type of problem, a conversation could go as follows:

He: *"I really get upset when Tracey [using her name instead of the more offensive 'your daughter'] leaves the bathroom a mess."*

She: *"She can be rather messy, but she is a teenager."*

He: *"I realize that, but I can never find anything and the towels are usually on the floor. Can we figure out a solution to this?"*

She: *"Maybe Tracey should just use the bathroom downstairs and she can be completely responsible for cleaning it up once a week."*

He: *"That sounds better. Let's discuss it with her."*

These "I" statements also work well in talking with children, particularly when they are teenagers. Teens are very prone to jumping on the defensive side, and that generally leads to an argument, as well. Utilizing non-threatening opening statements instead of immediately going into attack mode can prevent this.

Another effective communication technique involves leaving the house if highly emotional issues need to be discussed. Instead of remaining at home, where voices can be raised with impunity, going to a family restaurant or coffee shop can ensure that the discussion stays quiet and calm.

No one wants to be embarrassed in public, so an extra effort will usually be made by both parties to keep their voices down. Whenever a conversation starts with "We need to talk about _____." [insert an emotional issue], then it is time for a frappuccino at the local café. This technique has the added advantage of giving the couple some time alone. Many couples will argue that they don't have time to do this, but the consequence for not taking the time can be a strained marriage.

The difficulties involved in stepparenting and blending families can lead to many emotionally charged topics that will have to be dealt with, especially in the first years of the marriage, and these issues will be much easier to solve if effective communication techniques are used to avoid fighting over sensitive or difficult issues.

Maintaining a strong marriage should be a priority for all newlyweds, but there are special challenges in stepparenting that make this even more important. Since most couples do not initially realize the nature and complexity of the problems that they will face in the early days of their marriage, especially with regard to stepchildren, they often do not focus on marital issues until difficulties are encountered.

Potential Problem Areas

There are several key problem areas unique to stepparenting that plague remarriages. These issues have to be anticipated, or at least identified very early in the marriage, if they are to be prevented from seriously affecting the relationship. While those involving the stepchildren will be dealt with in the next chapter, there are still two major problem areas that need to be anticipated and prepared for.

Unresolved Grief

Whenever anger or the anger produced by guilt from a previous relationship remains unresolved, then remarriages will be in danger. While the emotions may be directed mainly at the former spouse, they will inevitably spill over into the new marriage and lead to unnecessary arguments and battles. The situation is similar to someone who has a difficult day at work and then comes home and takes his or her frustrations out on the spouse. The anger at the former spouse, whether because of that person's antagonistic behaviour or from guilt feelings resulting from your own part in the family break-up, cannot help but interfere with the new relationship.

This interference takes the form of being constantly on edge, so that a glass left on the coffee table by a youngster or a casual comment by the spouse that you look tired can result in an explosion far out of proportion to the actual significance of the event. The continual tension that this unresolved grief can cause will act like an abrasive on the relationship and gradually wear it down. Both parties need to be aware of the potential danger that lurks here, recognize it when it happens, and seek counselling help as soon as possible.

Ex-Spousal Interference

Similar to a marital partner who has unresolved grief issues, an angry ex-spouse can also set a family on edge. The harassing tactics and frustrations imposed by such a person can seriously strain a marriage unless both partners work together to counteract these effects. There is nothing that can be done about the ex, but there are ways to diminish the potentially harmful consequences that an angry and vengeful former partner can have on a new marriage.

The first step is for both parties in the new marriage to recognize the possible dangers of this person. Tactics such as failure to pay child support, refusals to change weekends when necessary, frequent complaining telephone calls, or refusal to communicate at all can be wearing on a relationship. Recognition that the ex-spouse is likely to present a problem is the first step in being able to deal with him or her effectively.

Once the problem is recognized, a common front can be maintained against any possible harmful effects that these childish tactics can cause.

SCOTT WOODING

The only effective approach is a steadfast refusal by both newlyweds to react in kind or to let themselves succumb to anger and frustration. The attitude that needs to be adopted—and this takes considerable practice—is that the ex has the problem; we don't. While this may seem appropriate only for such saints as Mother Teresa, it actually can be done by anyone, especially when both spouses are supporting each other. Retaliation in any way will only prolong the struggle and further feed the ex-spouse's fury. The biblical response of turning the other cheek may be too high a standard to attain, but refusing to respond will eventually have the effect of the behaviour's being extinguished. The greater the anger (or emotional disturbance in many cases), the longer this extinguishing process will take, but have faith—it will work eventually.

It is an unfortunate fact of life that remarriages involving children are far more complex than first marriages. However, if these difficulties are recognized and planned for, then they quickly disappear and an almost normal family structure can be developed.

Chapter 4

Building the Stepfamily

A newly married couple's relationship is rarely a problem, even when children from a previous relationship are involved. They are in love and life is good. The real problem is usually between the stepparents and stepchildren in these new marriages. They have to form a bond with each other if the marriage is to continue past the honeymoon period and that is almost always a tremendous challenge. If all the steps outlined in Chapter 2 have been followed so that a relationship has already been formed with the children, then the transition to living with these kids may be relatively easy, with only a few minor adjustments to make. Unfortunately, this is rarely the case. Most stepparents enter the relationship blindly expecting that because the children's parent loves them, the kids will automatically love them, too. Nothing is further from the truth.

The reality is that most stepchildren resent their new "parent" for a number of reasons, including:

- Unresolved grief from the break-up of their biological parents. They want their old home life back.
- Fears that their parent's new spouse will try to replace the estranged biological parent and they won't see their mother or father anymore.

- Resentment that the new spouse will take priority over them in the new family, especially if they've lived with their single parent for a number of years.
- If the new spouse has children, resentment that they no longer are the centre of their biological parent's attention.

Just one of these is enough to set a stepchild on edge, making the child suspicious and resentful of the newcomer; combined they can be lethal.

Why so many prospective stepparents are so naive is a mystery. Everyone knows about Cinderella, the fairy tale that made "evil" step-mothers a cliché. On a more contemporary level, the Harry Potter books show how devastating to a child an inconsiderate or uncaring stepparent(s) can be. While no one goes into a marriage intending to be such a parent, few people use these literary examples to understand how devastating a poor stepparenting relationship can be, and consequently, take steps to avoid such a relationship. Those who do enter a relationship involving children, and who are concerned about not becoming an "evil" stepparent, often overreact by trying too hard to be kind and considerate and end up alienating the children in another way.

It almost seems like a no-win situation, but this is definitely not true. If a potential stepparent has a full understanding of the difficulties of rais-ing someone else's children, and understands what steps need to be taken to avoid becoming Cinderella's stepmother, then success can almost be guaranteed. Unfortunately a number of myths about stepfamilies are float-ing throughout the marital ether and these fabrications often blind poten-tial stepparents to the difficulties of the process. The first step in the process of bonding with stepchildren in order to build a strong stepfamily is to examine and explode these myths.

Stepfamily Myths

The origin of these fables about stepfamilies, like the origin of all myths, is lost in time. Suffice it to say that they are indeed fables. They are not true, and believing them seriously lengthens the bonding process of a newly minted stepfamily. These are the main myths:

- **Stepfamilies are nuclear families.** Unfortunately this can never be true. The biological bonds that exist in a nuclear family are not all present in a stepfamily. A stepparent has not been present from birth and can never have the same relationship that a biological parent can. However, prospective stepparents need not despair. An excellent relationship can definitely be formed, given time and effort, and this relationship can be rewarding and enjoyable—it just will never be quite the same as that with a natural parent.

- **Stepchildren should bond immediately with their stepparents.** "Crikey!" (as Steve Irwin, the Crocodile Hunter, used to say). Whoever started this myth should be shot at sunrise. While every family will be different, complete bonding, involving the love and respect of all family members, can be expected to take years. This is a far cry from immediately. This does not mean that the entire family will be at war for years. On the contrary, with understanding and effort, most of the process can be relatively peaceful. It's just that the love and caring for each other that most nuclear families enjoy from birth (but which can nevertheless be easily destroyed), will take several years to fully develop. Patience is not just a virtue in this process, it is a requirement.

- **All family members will instantly love and respect each other.** This myth is an extension of the previous one and pertains especially to blended families. Parents cannot assume that their children are going to bond with their spouse's kids immediately. This can happen, but it is extremely rare. Competitions for attention, cries of favouritism, rivalries, and privacy violations can all be expected to occur in a blended family. These issues will be discussed in more detail in a later chapter. For now it is sufficient to simply understand that the kids will need time and a lot of family meetings if they are ever to bond with each other. It definitely will not happen just because their parents married each other.

- **Part-time stepfamilies are easier.** These are families where the children live with their other biological parent and only visit periodically. Many think that because the visits are intermittent, they will be easier to deal with. Once again, this is a myth. If anything, the process of bonding with the children is even harder because there is less time available to get to know them and for them to get to know you. In other words, the process will take even longer than normal and require considerably more patience and understanding than it would if the children lived with you and just visited the other biological parent. Again, the bonding can happen with some hard work, but the time for this to occur can effectively be doubled in most cases.

It is important to understand that these misconceptions are indeed myths, not to discourage anyone from stepparenting, but so that the anger and disappointment that can result from believing them can be avoided. These negative emotions that can develop from the realities of step parenting can result in another of those vicious circles. This one looks something like this:

Stepparent enters family thinking all members will bond instantly

↓

Stepparent discovers children are angry and resentful

↓

Stepparent responds with disappointment and anger

↓

Stepchildren react with antagonism
to stepparent's anger and resentment

↓

As this pattern continues, the gulf between stepparent and stepchildren gets wider and wider. It is vital that the vicious circle never get started, and this is only possible if prospective stepparents understand that the process is unique and takes time and effort on their part. It is also vital that the natural resentment that most stepchildren have to their situation not be taken personally. This will be discussed further in a later section.

The Stages of Stepparenting

While every family's circumstance is different, most will follow a similar pattern of development consisting of four main stages. The differences will be in how long each family remains in a particular stage. The ideal would be to move through them as quickly as possible in order to reach a state resembling a nuclear family where peace, harmony, love, and respect are exhibited most of the time.

Stage 1 – The Honeymoon Period

This stage can be confusing for most stepparents, especially those who believe in the myths described above. In this stage the newlywed parents are blissful, having just returned from their real honeymoon, so they are calm and relaxed. The children are probably not in a blissful state at all, but are in a holding pattern, waiting to see how things turn out. During this period, the kids are usually respectful of their biological parent's happiness and try hard not to cause any disturbances.

This stage is similar to the "Phony War" early in the Second World War, the period of about eight months after the declaration of war during which no battles actually took place. Both sides were building up their forces and planning strategies, and, as a result, nothing was happening. The potential for conflict was there, simmering under the surface, just as it is in new stepfamilies. If the parents, happily wrapped in the mythology of stepparenting, do not take any preventative action, warfare can erupt. During this stage, the stepparents need to work hard at developing a relationship with the children. A good relationship might not prevent Stage 2, but it will shorten it.

Stage 2 – The Testing Period

During this stage, reality sets in. This is when the children begin exhibiting behaviours that reflect their anger and resentment over their situation

SCOTT WOODING

in life. They usually do not want to be stepparented and display actions that signal their displeasure, including:

- **Divide and Conquer.** Children have been using this age-old strategy for years: if dad doesn't agree, go to mother, or vice versa. If the parents aren't communicating effectively, this tactic works well. The tactic can be even more effective with a stepparent. It goes something like this:

Stepchild:	*"Can I sleep over at Martha's tonight?"*
Stepmother:	*"No. It's a school night."*
Stepchild:	*"Dad always lets me stay at Martha's on weeknights. We do our homework together."*
Stepmother:	*"Really?"*
Stepchild:	*"Oh, yeah. We do it all the time."*

  Very often the stepparent, in this case a stepmother, is loath to upset the stepchild and so does not check with the father. Perhaps the father might be out of town or at work, so checking is difficult. In any case, the technique can be effective, not only for getting the child what she wants, but also creating tension between the stepmother and the father—when he finds out his daughter has been allowed a sleepover on a weeknight, the father may be upset with the stepmother, which often suits the child very well.

- **"You're not my real parent; you can't tell me what to do!"** This, too, is a time-honoured tactic on the part of stepchildren, who will often use it when they are thwarted by the stepparent in what they want to do, or when they are reminded of a chore they didn't do. The idea here is to put the stepparent on the defensive as well as to show displeasure not only for the actions of the moment, but possibly for the marriage as well. The sad fact is that this tactic works all too often. Most stepparents are horrified to hear this statement and react angrily, getting into the vicious circle described above.

This statement is a part of a policy of open hostility that some stepchildren will take toward a stepparent. While frustrating, at least it makes it obvious that the child is upset, and steps can be taken to find a solution to the child's anger.

- **Passive-aggressive actions.** Passive-aggressive behaviour is resistance to following parental instructions that takes the form of antipathy, stubbornness, procrastination, sullenness, or repeated failure to accomplish assigned tasks. This type of behaviour is very common among stepchildren as a way to display their displeasure with the parent's marriage. There is no apparent defiance, just an annoying lack of compliance, an ignoring of instructions. It can also take the form of the child staying long hours in his or her room or using other methods of avoiding contact with the stepparent.

Note:
Failure to do chores is not always passive-aggressive behaviour. If the children are teenagers, they will usually have trouble with fulfilling their duties. A later chapter will detail the special problems that teens present, not just for stepparents, but also for parents in general.

It is how the parents react to this testing period that can set the tone for the entire stepparenting relationship. If this period is expected and a strategy developed ahead of time to deal with it, then the period will be relatively short. If, instead, the parents take the behaviour personally and react with anger, then it may end only when the children leave home.

Stage 3 – The Truce

This stage, which marks the end of the testing period, usually sneaks up on the parents; there is rarely a definitive moment when it begins. A stepparent might hear a statement like, "You know, you're not so bad after all," but this is rare. More commonly, parents will suddenly realize that the stepchildren are no longer battling. This stage is so subtle that the truce may have been happening for several months before it is noticed.

While not necessarily the end to hostilities, a truce is a step in the right direction. Problems may still occasionally surface, but if the parents react to the truce with thanks and praise for jobs well done, and if the stepparent can now relax more with the children, then this stage will quickly move to the next level.

Stage 4 – Love and Respect

This is the stage all stepparents want to get to. It is the one that, in their naïveté, they expected in the first place. It is at this point that the occasional "I love you" may be heard, or the stepchild may spontaneously slip in a "mom" or "dad." It is certainly the plateau when peace and harmony generally exist in the family. Some estimates for the time it takes to reach this level range as high as seven years. Of course, it does not have to take this long. If the stepparent works at the bonding process, as detailed in the next section, and if the biological parent is working together with his or her spouse, then the time to reach this stage can be shortened considerably.

Bonding with Stepchildren

Ideally this process should begin well before the marriage, but unfortunately the great majority of prospective stepparents don't realize that it is necessary. The truth is that it is always necessary for the prospective or de facto stepparent to take the initiative in the bonding process. The stepchildren will almost always be angry and upset with the idea of their parent marrying. Remember that marriage destroys the great dream—that the biological parents will someday get back together. As outlined in Chapter 2, the following are some of the fears that children have when their parent remarries, often causing them to be on edge and defensive with the stepparent:

a) That to accept a new person is a betrayal of their other biological parent.

b) Are they being disloyal to this parent? Will he or she be upset with them if they tolerate this new family member?

c) That this new person might replace them as their parent's friend and confidant, or replace them as number one in the parent's heart.

d) That their parent might get hurt again just as he or she was by the divorce.

These fears have to be understood by a stepparent. They are very real and very frightening to children. Often the kids themselves do not fully understand the origins of their hostility to a stepparent, but it is usually rooted in these fears or in the explosion of their great dream. The key is to realize that it is not you as a person that the kids resent—it is what you represent. When this fact is absorbed, the new stepparent can relax and not take the testing behaviours of the children personally.

This is the real key to stepparenting. If the behaviours resulting from the children's fears and worries are taken personally, it is impossible to relax with them. The stepparent will constantly be on edge and will react defensively to the hostility and defiance that they see in the kids. When this happens, that vicious circle begins. This cannot be allowed to develop, and it won't if the stepparent takes the time and effort to understand the reasons for the children's negative behaviour and then takes some of the following actions to work through it.

1. Keep Calm.

    No matter what tests the kids put you through, no purpose will be served by getting angry. You may have to impose consequences for misbehaviour, but it is vital that you don't lose your cool while doing so. Once again, you are being asked for saintliness, but the importance of being cool and rational cannot be understated. Anger in a stepparent usually results from assuming that the children are doing these things to you personally. This is far from the truth—they would do similar things to Hilary Duff if she were their stepmother. Just relax and assume that the children are scared and worried. It is up to the stepparent to do everything possible to reduce these fears.

2. Show an Interest in Them.

    This is easy if the new stepparent likes children and can naturally relax with them, but much more difficult for someone who is initially hesitant and unsure of themselves. The idea is to display a genuine interest in the activities and interests of the children. This can be done in a number of ways. The first is to find out as much as possible about these interests. If a girl is enjoying her dance classes, find out about what kind of dance she likes, where her studio is, and who her teacher is. Dance is a relatively easy activity to explore for stepmothers, but may be more of a challenge to stepdads, as dance is not something they intrinsically understand. A stepson's mountain biking, on the other hand, may be easier for a stepfather to absorb, but more challenging for a stepmother. No matter, it is vital to learn as much as possible about these activities in order to share the stepchild's enthusiasm.

The next step is to learn to question the child about their activities. In other words, ask how it's going, what they are taking in their lessons, what is hard or difficult for them, or even get them to explain in some detail what they are talking about. Here are a couple of sample conversations to highlight this process.

Stepmother:	*"How was basketball practice today?"*
Stepson:	*"Fine." (Typical teenage response—more probing needed)*
Stepmother:	*"What were you guys working on?"*
Stepson:	*"Oh, the coach is putting in a new offence. It's kind of tricky to learn."*
Stepmother:	*"Sorry to show my ignorance, but what's an offence?"*
Stepson:	*"That's when we have the ball and are trying to score. We try different things to get someone free for a shot."*
Stepmother:	*"That sounds interesting. Can you show me how it works?"*

And the conversation is on. This one illustrates some key points about showing an interest. The first is that it usually takes two or three questions to get a conversation going, especially with teenagers. The second is that you don't have to know much about your stepchildren's activities. You can ask them to explain them initially. After that, it's important to remember what you have been told so that the kids know you really are interested. If you keep asking the same questions over and over, they think (probably rightly) that your interest isn't really genuine. Here is another sample.

Stepfather:	*"How was swimming today?"*
Stepdaughter:	*"It was fun."*
Stepfather:	*"Do you specialize in one stroke or do you do several?"*
Stepdaughter:	*"I mostly do freestyle and the 'fly."*
Stepfather:	*"What's the 'fly?"*
Stepdaughter:	*"It's the butterfly, when you stroke like this." (She demonstrates)*
Stepfather:	*"That looks interesting. Which one do you like better?"*

And once again the conversation continues. The interesting part of this conversation to note is that the stepfather had either done some homework or knew something about swimming. He knew there were different strokes and distances, just not the exact details of each stroke. It is always helpful to conversation and gratifying to a stepchild if the stepparent takes the time to find out about the hobby or sport. You don't have to know everything, just enough to show that you are interested. This is good advice for any parent but absolutely essential knowledge for a stepparent.

3. Attend Their Events.

    This is an extension of showing an interest. It is hard for the stepchild to believe you are really interested if you do not attend games, recitals, and shows. These two concepts, showing an interest and attending events, are an important combination in the bonding process. Many stepchildren regard a stepparent who only attends events, as being phony because interest has not been shown on a day-to-day basis. The opposite is also true. Just asking questions and displaying an interest without actually attending the events is not enough to convince a stepchild that your interest is genuine. You must do both.

It is important to understand that attending events should be automatic. Don't ask the child if he or she wants you to attend. They will almost always say it doesn't matter. This is especially true of teenagers. They need to be cool and independent—it's part of the adolescence process. Just go to the events and discuss them afterwards. At the events it is not necessary to overdo it by cheering the loudest or yelling at the referee; it's enough just to be there.

4. Share Your Interests.

Another way of developing a bond with a stepchild is to get them involved in your own hobbies or interests. This has to be done carefully—it cannot be forced, but often stepchildren will be excited not only by the hobby or activity itself, but by the fact that the stepparent is taking the time to explain the activity and to participate in it with the stepchild. While a passion for stamp collecting or chess may not work with many teenagers, it will be of interest to some. Mountain biking, motorcycling, sailing, or drag racing will more than likely hold most boys' interest—and some girls, too. Other girls may be interested in a stepmother's enjoyment of golf, tennis, quilting, or painting. It never hurts to try to get them interested, and it may provide a great bonding tool.

Another advantage of sharing these interests is that the child sees the stepparent in a different setting. Outside the home, in a setting where the stepparent is relaxed and discipline is not usually required, the stepkids see a totally different side of you. Relaxed settings are also where conversations flow much more easily; the trip to the driving range may be a great time to catch up on the details of the children's lives.

5. Treat Them Like Your Own.

This is the great secret to the process. It is an easy thing to say but much more complicated to do. What treating them like your own involves is an unconditional, positive acceptance of the stepchildren right from day one. It is a relaxed and calm approach that welcomes and accepts even the most recalcitrant child. This approach comes easily to those who like children, and it is much easier to use when the kids are not openly hostile. No matter what the kids are like, the welcome and ensuing approach must be the same. You must show that you like them and are pleased to be their parent.

This unconditional acceptance has to be genuine because you can't fool kids. They can feel fear, tension, or hostility and will respond in kind. Just don't be surprised if even this attitude does not seem to work at first. It will take time to overcome the children's fears and concerns about having a new stepparent. Usually this time is measured in years, but the "treat them like your own" approach will minimize the hostility so that love and respect can follow eventually. The advantage to this attitude is that no one can continue to dislike someone who obviously likes them.

Casey's parents split up when she was three. Her dad moved to another town, about a hundred kilometres away, and her mother retained primary custody. Traveling back and forth was time-consuming and her mother refused to drive her daughter all that way every two weeks. Casey's father, Dave, was not deterred and drove to pick her up on Friday every two weeks, then drove her home on Sundays. After a couple of years, Dave remarried a woman with two children. Casey's mother had several boyfriends but did not remarry.

When Casey was 10, her mother had another daughter with her live-in boyfriend. This relationship was tumultuous, but the boyfriend did not mistreat her. During one visitation, Casey voiced the desire to come and live with her father and stepmother. This was a huge surprise to Dave as Casey was a very quiet and shy girl and had never given any indication of wanting to come and live with them before. Accordingly, Dave began the process of trying to get primary custody, which, quite predictably, the mother opposed.

She maintained that Dave had brainwashed Casey and poisoned her against her mother.

Dave then took Casey to a counsellor to get his opinion on whether or not his daughter was being unduly pressured to come and live with him and his wife and stepdaughters. The counsellor was somewhat amazed to find that Casey did indeed want to live with Dave. There was obviously no coercion occurring, but still, this was a massive decision for a shy, quiet 10-year-old to make: leave her mother, her school, her friends, and her baby stepsister to live in a new town with her dad and stepmother.

When asked why she was willing to do all this, Casey said that her stepmother treated her like her own child. She talked to her, showed an interest in her activities, and quite obviously liked her. The home was a loving and stable one, and she enjoyed this atmosphere. In contrast, her biological mother was frequently critical, had many boyfriends, and was often away from home, leaving Casey to babysit.

It is highly unusual for a child to want to leave the mother's home to live with a stepmother and stepsiblings, but this stepmother obviously had the right stuff. She was able to make a shy girl, who was probably initially terrified about going to an unfamiliar home setting, feel loved and accepted. While the stepmother's attitude may have been the result of a natural love of all children, it is one that can be adopted by any prospective stepparent who is willing to try.

Dealing with Initial Rejection

These bonding techniques are usually effective but they take time. This time can be measured in months if they are followed, if the divorce has been relatively amicable, and if Saturn remains in conjunction with Venus. However, it could also take years before the Love and Respect Stage is reached and that means a long period of time in the Testing Stage. No matter how patient a person you may be, years of hostility, whether overt or in passive form, can wear you down. Worse, they can seriously strain your marriage. To minimize this stress until the relatively peaceful stages of a stepfamily are reached, there are some strategies that should be followed.

The first strategy is to realize, then constantly to remind yourself that the kids are not doing this on purpose or to you in particular. Their hostility is not personal; it's just a result of their fears and their resentment of the situation they have been placed in by life. The fact that you didn't cause this situation is irrelevant to them. They're scared, confused, and angry and you present a convenient target. This may not be fair, but it's a fact of life that you must deal with if the family is ever to harmonize. The kids are too young and immature to rationalize their feelings and to realize that you are not the cause of their problems. They don't have any idea why they don't like you or why they are being rude or unkind to you. The roots of their behaviour are in their subconscious. The end result is that it is left to you to understand the kids and to deal with their negative emotions. This is much easier if you keep telling yourself, "It's not personal. They're not doing this on purpose." This mantra helps you to relax and deal with the problem more rationally.

A second strategy for dealing with stepchild hostility is to work in close harmony with the biological parent when dealing with disciplinary issues, rudeness, or other forms of hostility. This seems like a relatively easy request since that parent just happens to be your newly minted spouse. Unfortunately, life often doesn't work that way. There are many different reasons why this straightforward strategy is difficult to apply. These include the following:

- **Different Parenting Backgrounds and Philosophies**.
  Parents who come from homes with different parenting systems are a common problem when raising any children, but it becomes even more of a problem for stepparents. If one parent believes in a relatively strict approach to parenting, involving rules and consequences for

breaking them, while the other believes that kindness and reason are more effective, then problems are sure to occur. In any potential disciplinary situation the kids will run to the kinder, gentler parent and the divide-and-conquer problem will probably result. More detail on effective disciplinary approaches will be outlined in a later chapter, but for now, suffice it to say that it is critical that parents be on the same disciplinary page.

When Ted and Samantha got married, she already had a four-year-old son, Jason, by a previous relationship. Jason was an extremely active lad. Ted had come from a family that was very strict and structured, and so he was constantly reprimanding Jason for his rowdy behaviour. Samantha was in agreement that rules and structure were necessary, but was worried that Jason had already been through a divorce and needed more love and support than discipline. Whenever Ted would discipline the child, Jason would immediately run to his mother, who would plead his case. This became such a source of friction to the marriage that the couple sought counselling.

The problem was twofold. Ted was spending more time trying to "correct" Jason's behaviour than he was in trying to form a relationship with the child. He was convinced that the lad needed more discipline before he would earn the right to have fun with his new stepfather. Samantha saw that this hard-line approach was actually increasing the distance between her son and Ted, and so tended to try to compensate by being far too lenient with Jason. This leniency infuriated Ted, who generally reacted by being even stricter with Jason. The counsellor worked with the couple to find a more middle-of-the-road approach to discipline, with Ted becoming more relaxed and Samantha being less of a pushover. At the same time, Ted needed some strategies for bonding with Jason. Once these two areas were addressed, the marital battles ceased and Ted and Jason began getting along much better.

- **His, Hers, and Ours.**

There are many variations on this theme, such as, she has a child from a previous marriage and then the couple has children of their own; he has a child of his own; or both have kids from earlier relationships and then they have children together. Whatever the situation, the potential exists for differing treatment of the children. As one father said after several years in a blended family situation, "You can take more from your own kids than you can from someone else's." This sums up the situation perfectly. It is difficult for even the most motivated parents to treat all children in the family as if they were his or her own. As hard as this may be, it is important that both parents work closely together to see that it happens as often as possible. Family meetings can help this situation by airing concerns and by providing a forum to find solutions to these concerns.

One step that the parents must take—together—is to announce a baby's impending birth in discussion format, rather than just saying "Guess what? You're going to have a baby brother or sister!" The parents should sit down with the family, make the announcement, then discuss how the child or children might feel about this. Some will actually be able to say, "But I won't be the baby anymore," or "Will you still love me, too?" On the other hand, they may not say much at all, which will be the parents' clue to answer these questions even though they weren't asked.

It would be very easy to assume that all children will want a new sibling. Many won't. These will be the quieter, shyer, more fearful children, who need more than the average amount of attention and support. It is best for parents to pay close attention initially to the feelings of any children from a previous relationship, and then, once the baby is born, continue to monitor the situation for signs of jealousy or concern about their place in the family. Fairness to children becomes difficult, for example, when a stepchild is involved in a controversy with a biological child. All too often it is the biological child who gets the break. This may be because an "ours" child is younger, because the stepchild is more active and therefore always in trouble, or because there actually is favouritism occurring. No matter the reason, both parents must have frequent discussions about the children and heed the concerns raised at the family meetings.

- **Uninvolved Biological Parents.**
This is a strange variation on the stepparenting theme, but it happens all too often, usually with biological fathers. In this situation, the biological parent, happy to find a spouse who loves children and is obviously good to his kids, backs out of the parenting situation and leaves all the decision-making and day-to-day decisions to the stepparent. This puts a massive burden onto the stepparent. As capable as she might be, there will be that initial resentment to overcome and, instead of fading with time, this resentment will build when she inevitably handles situations in a way that the stepchild does not like. In this situation, the kids do not even have their own parent to appeal to when they are dissatisfied. This is unfair to both the children and the stepparent.

James was a tall, gangly 16-year-old when he was first brought in to see the counsellor. His mother had died two years previously and his father had remarried. The problem was that James was doing very poorly in school and did not seem to have any ambition to change this situation. His father was a busy medical doctor and his stepmother, Katherine, had been one of his nurses.

After conversation with all concerned it was obvious that Katherine was an excellent stepmother. She had efficiently taken over running the family and was well liked by James and his three older sisters. Unfortunately, liking Katherine was obviously not enough. James lacked confidence in himself and needed the support of a biological parent. Katherine was doing an excellent job but was not James's mother. He liked her, but she was still a relative stranger.

The counsellor suggested that his father spend more time with James doing activities that would bolster his low self-confidence. Both liked working on cars, and they had an old car at home that needed work, and both enjoyed flying. Dad agreed that this would be feasible. Unfortunately it never happened. Once the father left the counsellor's office, he resumed his busy practice and continued to leave the raising of his son to his wife. James's marks continued to fall, despite the help of an excellent tutor. Even with the counsellor and tutor working together, the dad remained aloof from the parenting situation.

The influence of a father on a young boy is huge. In this case, James had been hit with the double whammy of being shy and awkward and of losing his mother at a crucial stage in his life. Katherine did an excellent job of caretaking but could not meet his emotional needs. His dad should have been there for him but was not. As a result, the problem worsened: James and Katherine began to fight frequently and he eventually moved out of the house. He did not attend post-secondary school, as his marks were not high enough despite his obvious intelligence. His dad and his stepmother needed to work together to help James overcome his confidence issues and it just never happened.

- **Uninvolved Stepparent.**

This is a more common circumstance, once again mainly with stepfathers, but which can occur with either parent. In this case, the stepparent backs out of the parenting situation and leaves everything to the biological parent. This usually occurs with stepparents who are not naturally good with children and who feel awkward with them, or those who have never had children of their own and who are presented with older children. While they might be good parents of their own children, they do not feel comfortable with someone else's, and they withdraw from taking an active part in raising these kids. This situation often results in problems similar to that of James in the above example. Boys and girls need a relationship with a parent of their own sex in order to develop a positive self-image, and when one is not available, their self-confidence suffers. Stepparents need to work hard on bonding with the spouse's children to provide a positive same-sex influence. Some may try but get discouraged when they meet the usual initial resistance to their presence. Others just never try. This is very hard on the children and makes their adjustment to the original divorce almost impossible.

It is crucial that the biological parent and the stepparent work closely together to help the stepparent overcome the initial rejection that he or she might experience and get out of the Testing Stage as fast as possible. If this does not appear to be happening, then counselling should be sought immediately. This is too important for everyone to just ignore the problems and hope they will go away. They don't. They fester, get worse, and everyone suffers as a result.

When stepparents meet the initial rejection that so often accompanies their marriage, most react with frustration and anger. They do not expect it and they have not taken any steps to form a relationship with the child. This rejection should be expected and not be reacted to with disappointment and anger. It is up to the stepparent, supported by the biological parent, to work hard to overcome a stepchild's initial negative emotions—not the other way round. The stepchild simply does not have the maturity and life experience to understand the behaviours of the adults in their world and to adjust to these. As long as this is understood by all adults involved and they work together to overcome the early resistance, then good things will eventually happen. Patience and persistence will overcome a stepchild's original scepticism of their stepparent.

Battling the Ex-Spouse

If stepparents are ever to bond with their stepchildren, they must not get drawn into the battle that may be ongoing between their current partner and an ex-spouse. This doesn't mean that they can't support their spouse by helping to reduce the agony of these clashes. But it does mean that they will not endear themselves to their stepchildren if they actively join the fight. No matter how big an idiot the ex-spouse may appear, he or she is still the parent of the stepchildren and the kids will still love that person. How these exes relate to their children is often completely different to how they relate to their former spouse. Getting into the fray may be tempting, but it is a very bad idea. Stepparents need to stay in the background on this issue or they will have great difficulty ever forming a close relationship with their stepchildren.

When Nothing Works

If you have followed all these steps to try and bond with your stepchild for several years and nothing has worked, then it is time to seek counselling. Even if you see no progress after a year, it would be a good idea to ask for help, though this is relatively early in the bonding process. There are a number of possibilities why the bonding process may not be happening that are outside even the most diligent of stepparent's control. These include:

* **Emotional Disturbance in the Child.**
  Conditions ranging from ADHD to more serious concerns such as antisocial personality disorder and bipolar disorder can critically affect the bonding process. This only happens in a small percentage of cases—professional estimates have it at two to five percent. However, these situations can occur. When nothing seems to be working, do not hesitate to seek help. One sign that emotional problems may be at the

root of a problem might be that there are no problems bonding with other stepchildren. If all seems to be going well with one or more of the other children, then sometimes it can be the child's problem and not that of the stepparent. Just don't assume this to be the case until you have worked hard at the bonding process with the stepchild.

- **Negative Influence of an Ex-Spouse.**
Some exes never grow up. They can often allow their break-up baggage to spill over onto their children to the point that they are actively sabotaging the relationship between them and their new stepparent. This situation is extremely difficult to do anything about, as it is the ex that needs the counselling and not the kids or you. Once again, patience and persistence will be the only answer. Stepparents need to don their "Mother Teresa" sainthood clothes and hang in there for the long term. The good news is that you can't fool kids for long. If the stepparent is trying hard, likes kids, and stays calm and caring, then the stepchildren will come around eventually. It's asking a lot of the stepparent, but it is vital to realize that when you married, you got the entire package, including the evil ex-spouse.

- **Interfering Grandparents.**
Amazingly, grandparents can sabotage the bonding process as effectively as their children can. They may blame their child's ex, now your spouse, for the break-up, and they can't let go themselves. This topic will be discussed in a later chapter, but it is another circumstance where direct intervention is impossible. You just have to grin and bear it until the kids get old enough or mature enough to realize where the problem really lies. They will, but these old folks can sometimes cause an amazing amount of grief in the short term.

While it is usually up to the stepparent to form a bond with their step-kids, it is not always the parent's fault when this does not happen. External factors can play a part in these situations. Fortunately, all they will usually do is delay the bonding process. Disturbed individuals cannot be allowed to distract a stepparent from the main goal of enjoying their new family. If they are allowed to interfere, then not only will the bonding suffer, so will the marriage itself. This is too serious a consequence, and both the stepparent and biological parent will have to work hard to avoid reacting in kind to these mentally unhealthy people.

Steps to Bonding with a Stepchild

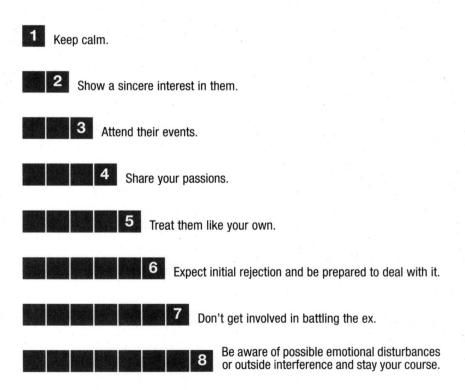

1 Keep calm.

2 Show a sincere interest in them.

3 Attend their events.

4 Share your passions.

5 Treat them like your own.

6 Expect initial rejection and be prepared to deal with it.

7 Don't get involved in battling the ex.

8 Be aware of possible emotional disturbances or outside interference and stay your course.

Chapter 5

"You're not my real parent—you can't tell me what to do!"

Few issues in a remarriage are as volatile as that of discipline. It is a key factor in any marriage, as disagreements about disciplining children can split a marriage almost as quickly as financial disagreements can. But this issue becomes even more important in a remarriage involving children because a key element in the disciplinary process is not there for stepparents to rely on. This element is the natural bond that exists between biological parents and their children. This bond, whether you call it love or attachment, is essential in establishing parental authority. Children love their parents and want to please them. This helps the children to accept discipline, as they usually know they have done something wrong and are unhappy that they have displeased their parents. This knowledge doesn't make them pleased to be receiving consequences for their actions, but it does help them to accept these consequences.

Stepparents do not have this bond to rely on; at least not for the first few years. Children are not concerned that their behaviour has displeased this new person in their lives. In fact, if the children are experiencing the emotions that have been described in earlier chapters, they may even believe that they are being loyal to their displaced biological parent by aggravating the new one. This means that a stepparent is automatically handicapped in the area of discipline. It will be harder for stepchildren to accept their authority and, as a result, a stepparent needs to be very careful about approaching this area.

Before discussing how stepparents should handle this thorny discipline issue, it is necessary to understand what discipline is and how it should be used in any family—not just the rebuilt kind.

Discipline in the New Millennium

Family discipline has undergone a revolution in the past few generations that has resulted in its being far more complex today than it ever was in the past. Prior to the 1950s discipline was simple. If a child misbehaved, a swat was applied, usually to the posterior and usually with the hand. This ended the matter. It did not take many of these swats to teach children either not to misbehave, or to be very careful about how they did it. Discipline was maintained. However, throughout the 1950s and 1960s, this process was examined by social authorities for its humaneness. They were concerned that corporal punishment did not do the job it was intended to do.

The purpose of discipline is to teach. The idea is to instruct children how to behave in society and how to avoid danger to themselves. Leaders in social thinking rightly felt that teaching should not be done through fear and pain, but through a system of reward and logical reasoning that supports this learning process. Under this more enlightened system, children were to be rewarded for behaving correctly, something that was rarely done in the "good old days," and given non-painful consequences when they misbehaved. This approach seemed very reasonable to most people but turned out to have many flaws.

THE "NEW" APPROACH TO DISCIPLINE

The following is a quote from a 1954 parenting manual entitled *Child Training: A Guide to Successful Parenthood*:

When the child is four or five, old enough to take some real responsibility for his behavior and to understand why he is being punished, punishment may occasionally be used effectively. It should not be necessary to punish a child frequently. If punishment is used often it is usually a sign that things are not going well between the parents and the youngster. Then it is time for the parents to think through the situation and try to find the cause of the trouble. _____

Statements such as these were very confusing to parents. First of all, how do you know when your child is ready for consequences? What should you do for the first four or five years? Are you resorting to punishment too often? There are so many questions that parents tended to be paralyzed lest they do the wrong thing and psychologically damage the child. The result of such vague and confusing statements has been that discipline has deteriorated badly in the past two generations to the point that in many families it does not actually exist at all.

The problem with the new discipline was that it was far too cumbersome and confusing for most parents. They were trying to explain to their children why they shouldn't be misbehaving when these children were far too young to understand the parental reasoning. The kids had no life experience to fall back on, so that when their parents said, "Don't go out on the road or a car might run over you and kill you," they simply didn't know what this meant. Explanations simply do not have the impact of a rapidly imposed consequence. The "experts" even decried the raising of the voice. Everything was supposed to be done in a calm and controlled tone of voice. Try that when your child has just destroyed your most precious crystal vase! If everything is said and done calmly, no sense of urgency or importance is conveyed to the child. The result for parents who tried this modern approach was that the negative behaviour did not stop.

At the same time, parents were afraid to impose punishments (this word is no longer allowed in modern parlance; "consequences" must be used instead) for fear that they would psychologically damage their children in some way. While the books all said that consequences could be used, they added so many restrictions and conditions that eventually many parents came to believe that they should not be used all.

That, in fact, is the attitude to discipline that is most pervasive today. Parents are afraid to raise their voices or impose any form of consequences on their children in the mistaken belief that this will harm them in some way. Bollocks! Nothing could be further from the truth. While there is never a need for hurting the child physically, conveying a sense of urgency by raising your voice, usually after an initial warning, is only reasonable. Similarly, it is usually vital that consequences be imposed for misbe-haviour. These can be as simple as depriving a young child of a toy or a teenager of computer use. They might involve a period of time in the child's room or a three-day cell-phone confiscation for a teenager. These must be imposed swiftly and, if possible, without anger. However, if a state of serenity is impossible, it will not be a deal breaker if a parent occasionally loses his or her cool.

The reality of discipline is that children need it and prefer it. A set of household rules backed up by consequences for breaking them gives children a sense of safety and security. Knowing where the boundaries are makes young children more comfortable. Older children, moreover, recognize that parents who utilize discipline are doing so because they care about them. This does not mean that they will thank you when a consequence is imposed, but it does mean that in the long run they will appreciate what has been done for them.

Brent was 14 when his mother first saw a psychologist about his refusal to obey her and his apparent lack of motivation. He was a gifted athlete but often did not go to practices or, occasionally, even to his games if his friends were doing something interesting. He also had a part-time job but just did not show up if he didn't feel like it. His marks were average but below what they could have been.

His mother was at her wit's end trying to get him to fulfill his commitments. His father had long ago washed his hands of the lad, saying that he was impossible to deal with. They would threaten not to pay for his league fees if he didn't attend practices or to ground him, but they never followed through.

The psychologist advised that the parents needed attention to two areas. First, it was obvious that Brent's self-image was very low. He was afraid to try at sports or school for fear of failure. Despite his obvious talents, he did not believe in himself. It was recommended that his father spend more time with him by attending his games, supporting his participation and accomplishments verbally, and by doing other recreational activities with him. This would have a major effect on his self-worth and would help him to move forward from his fear of trying.

The second recommendation was that both parents follow through on their disciplinary threats. They did not need to get angry with Brent, because the situation was not in any way his fault. Instead, they just needed to be consistent. If he failed to live up to a responsibility, he should lose a privilege. If he did not have any money, he should fulfill his job commitment, not receive it from his parents. It was also suggested that his mother, who was trying to fill the role of both parents and who felt guilty that his dad was not actively parenting, stop phoning the coach or Brent's employer to make excuses for him.

Two years later, the mother called the psychologist again. She was still having the exact same difficulties. When asked whether the family had implemented the suggestions, she ruefully admitted

that they had not. Brent had recently stayed home from an impor-
tant baseball game to hang out with his friends. He'd also had the
opportunity to work that day. When his mother had tried to insist
that he do one or the other, he'd gone to bed and stayed there all
day. Asked what she had done about this, the mom admitted that
she did nothing. She was afraid to do anything in case she further
alienated the lad. In fact, the opposite was true. She was causing
far more psychological damage by not enforcing some basic rules.
She was reinforcing Brent's feelings, which stemmed largely from
his father's lack of interest in him, that no one really cared about
him.

This is a typical modern family problem. Far too many parents are so confused about discipline that they don't realize that, no matter what other dynamics are at work in the family, it is still a vital component of child-raising. When other factors are at work—Brent's emotionally absent father, for example—discipline in its true form is critical to the children's feeling safe and secure and loved. This scenario is often played out in recently divorced families. The custodial parent often tries to make up for the family breakup, for which they usually feel at least partly responsible, by being lax about discipline, in the mistaken belief it will make the child feel better. The opposite is actually true. The children will continue any negative behaviours they may have developed, often subconsciously, to get the parent to pay attention to the real problem—whatever that may be. The kids will push the limits in an attempt to find where those limits actually are, in order to be reassured that their parent(s) really care about them. Sadly, most parents misinterpret these behaviours and either over-react, harshly and angrily, or do nothing for fear of doing the wrong thing.

SCOTT WOODING

The Importance of Family Backgrounds

One of the sad commentaries on our modern society is that there is no common forum where child-raising, including effective disciplinary techniques, can be taught. Certainly there are some (voluntary) prenatal classes where basic infant caretaking skills are dispensed, but after that—nothing. Some parents do read up on modern disciplinary theories and techniques (with the resulting confusion discussed above) but most parents do not seem to have time even for this relatively minor research. This is unfortunate because it means that instead of learning the most effective child-raising techniques, the only ones available are those learned from your own upbringing. For better or worse, this is all a parent has to fall back on when the inevitable disciplinary situations arise. Each family has a different approach, a fact that is particularly true in North America, where people come from such diverse ethnic and cultural backgrounds. The result is that when two people decide to marry and have children, their approaches to discipline may be radically different. One may be relatively relaxed and permissive, while the other parent may be a proverbial drill sergeant. This can cause a tremendous amount of friction in the best of marriages, most especially when a stepparent is involved.

The difference between a marriage with two biological parents and one with a stepparent is that bond that was mentioned earlier in the chapter. While there might not be a major problem if the biological parent is the strict one and the stepparent is relatively permissive (although there will still be problems), the reverse situation creates an immense barrier for the non-biological parent. The remarriage where the stepparent is stricter than the natural parent will have to expect difficulties. There will undoubtedly be acceptance problems for the children and even rebelliousness from them. Developing a warm and comfortable relationship with the stepchildren will be a long and tension-filled process if both parents do not have a common approach. Allen provides us with a perfect example of this.

Allen and Marla had been married for just over a year when the problems came to a head. Marla had two children by a previous marriage: a boy aged 12 and a 14-year-old girl, while Allen had never been married before. A period of five years had elapsed between the breakup of Marla's first marriage and her remarriage, allowing a very close relationship to develop between her and the children.

The major disagreements revolved around doing chores around the house. Allen was a tidiness fanatic who had no understanding of the disorganized nature of teenagers. Neither child was a disciplinary challenge; both did well in school and followed the household rules with few complaints. However, like so many adults, Allen could not grasp why they were not able to get a few simple chores done—and done correctly. He was constantly angry at the children for not doing the dishes, for leaving their clothing lying around, and for not cleaning the bathrooms. Marla tried to mediate but was caught between her love of Allen and her natural instinct to defend her children. She was much more casual about the house and, while she liked it to be tidy, did not get particularly upset when the kids didn't do their chores on time. She knew they were good kids, but Allen seemed constantly to portray them as lazy and indifferent.

The situation finally came to a head after a major argument, and counselling was sought. The main problem was twofold. The first was that Allen had come from a very strict household where indiscretions were immediately followed by physical consequences. While he did not ascribe to the physical part, the only disciplinary methods he knew were angry and harsh. The incident that brought this situation to a head was that, although the daughter had actually done her weekly bathroom cleaning on time, she had failed to dust the baseboards. Allen went ballistic and grounded her for a week. Marla defended her strongly, resulting in a vicious battle followed by Allen actually moving out for a week. He simply could not *relax and deal with the situation calmly. Perfection was all he knew.*

The second problem was that Allen, never having had kids of his own, not only knew nothing about raising them, he had no knowledge of the biological bond between parents and their children. By attacking her children, Allen did not realize that he was also attacking Marla, who had raised them herself for so long. She was able to keep silent for a while, but finally could not stand by and allow her children to be constantly reprimanded and punished. She knew they were good kids, but Allen did not. He had no experience in this area.

After several sessions, it became obvious that Allen simply did not get it. He could not overcome his family background and learn to be more tolerant. The marriage dissolved.

The above situation is a common one. Parents must be on the same page when it comes to discipline if conflict is to be avoided. This is doubly true for stepparenting situations. It is, as has been said, crucial to have a discipline within any family. The problem comes when there is a difference in what the standards are and how they are applied. If the stepparent is the stricter one, then it very often happens that the biological parent is placed in a situation of having to defend his or her own children. The result is that not only do they not agree on an approach to discipline, the arguments become a personal attack on the biological parent. At this point, either the standards get harmonized or the marriage could easily fall apart. Even if it doesn't, the children will have a very hard time developing a close relationship with this stepparent.

Anger Has No Place in Discipline

This topic was discussed earlier and is mentioned frequently in this book, but a brief recapitulation will serve to reinforce this vital concept. Anger is a powerful emotion that appears to have developed to protect people from their enemies and, as such, has little place in modern society. Anger makes people stronger and faster and shuts down the cognitive (thinking) portion of brain while the emotion is being experienced. The desire to hurt is uppermost while one is angry, and this would serve well if you had to fight off an enemy, but that would be a rare experience in our world. It has already been discussed in the above section that hurting should not be a part of the disciplinary process.

The sole purpose of discipline is to teach appropriate behaviour. Anger, then, must be avoided if effective discipline is to occur, because it must be reasonable rather than punitive. The thinking part of the brain needs to work in order to be able to decide whether consequences are needed and, what they should be. Not only that, but when anger occurs, it inevitably provokes emotion in the person who is the object of this anger. Young children will cry and be extremely upset, while teenagers may react defensively with anger in return. Since emotion interferes with learning, it is important that it not be produced in children who require discipline for their actions. They cannot learn the right lessons if they are upset. The formula needs to be: "This is what you did that was wrong. This is what you get for it. I love you."

That last brief statement in the formula is to indicate that the child's infraction of the rules has not resulted in a loss of affection on the parent's part. Anger will certainly give this impression. The idea is to convey that you are displeased by the action, not by the person. Being able to do this shows that the true purpose of discipline has been fully absorbed.

Stepparents absolutely must grasp this idea. They need to keep anger out of the situation much more than do biological parents. Rather than already having an emotional attachment with the children, stepparents are in the process of developing this attachment. Ineffective disciplinary techniques will interfere with the development of this relationship faster than anything else. There will be occasions when the biological parent is not available and the stepparent must deal with a situation. In these cases it is vital, especially in the early days of the marriage, that anger not be shown. It will only interfere with the disciplinary process as well as with bonding and developing a positive relationship with the children, which is vital for the success of the marriage.

Consequences

Parents are often confused as to what, if any, consequences should be administered when an infraction of the rules has occurred. Modern disciplinary theory often mentions "appropriate" consequences, meaning that they should result naturally from the action being disciplined. That is an excellent theory but is often virtually impossible to do. The difficulty comes from the fact that disciplinary actions are only effective if done immediately. This is true of all children, but especially true of the younger ones. If consequences are not applied immediately, they will not remember what it was that they did wrong, and the proper learning will not take effect.

This means that if parents cannot think of an appropriate consequence, one where the "punishment fits the crime," they may either hesitate too long for the discipline to be effective, or they may not give any consequences at all for fear of doing the wrong thing. What if they administer a consequence that is not appropriate to the infraction? Will the child get confused? Will there be psychological damage? Nuts—just do something. It does not actually matter what you do, as long as it is neither done in anger nor physical. What really matters is that action is taken immediately. The idea that it should be appropriate is nice, but is too difficult to administer. Any consequence will work as long as the child clearly knows what the infraction was. Just remember the disciplinary formula from the previous section and follow it religiously: "Here's what you did. Here's what you get for doing that. I love you."

So what consequences can a parent or stepparent use? One highly effective consequence is removal of a privilege such as television or video game use. Banishment to the bedroom for a specified period of time is another. This latter point is also important in administering consequences. They all should be time-limited. Indefinite consequences are frustrating for children—especially teenagers. Set a time limit for each one. It should go something like this: "You know that you weren't supposed to go to Johnny's house after school. There will be no television for you tonight. Sorry about that."

Another important point is that there is usually no need for long penalties. They become frustrating if they endure past their effective period. How long to make them is also a bit of an art, but they should range from a half-hour time out to three days for something really serious. Young children rarely need consequences that last more than a few hours at the very most. Their memories are very short and they will rarely remember what they did wrong past this time. Older children can absorb consequences that last longer for major infractions, such as missing curfew by an hour or more for no good reason. However, even teenagers don't need long consequences for most of their actions. Removing video-game privileges for even one day is usually enough for most of their "sins." For very serious mistakes, such as coming home drunk or shoplifting, it may be necessary to impose a consequence that lasts up to two weeks, but hopefully such circumstances will be rare and repeat offences will not occur, or counselling help may be necessary. As long as the imposition of a clear consequence is given for each infraction of the rules, then the message will be received that such misbehaviour will not be tolerated.

One consequence that should be avoided whenever possible is "grounding." This practice can be used, but it is fraught with dangers. One major problem technique is that the punishment period is usually not imposed immediately. For example, coming home from a party two hours late could be met with grounding for the next weekend. After all, grounding during the school week is rarely as much of a consequence as it would be on a weekend when the bulk of social activities take place. By the time

SCOTT WOODING

the punishment period rolls around, a week has passed and the child (usually a teenager) has usually forgotten what was so bad about what they did. They actually do have short memories during this time of life, especially when they don't really want to remember something. This results in the teen getting angry about not being able to go out, which puts a strain on everyone.

Another problem with grounding is that the parents are effectively grounded, too. They can't very well go out and leave their angry, grounded teenager at home. The temptations either to go out anyway or to invite some friends over are far too great, defeating the purpose of the consequence and possibly leading to more trouble. The parents may not have had any plans, but if they did, they will be ruined, as they have to stay home to supervise.

PARENTS NEED TO "STAY THE COURSE"

Here is an actual conversation witnessed by the author while visiting some friends:

Teen:	"Can I go over to Joey's?"
Mom:	"No. You're grounded."
Teen:	"Can I have some friends over then?"
Mom:	"No. I said you were grounded."
Teen:	"Well, I'd be staying home. I just want a couple of friends over."
Mom:	(weakening) "How many friends?"
Teen:	"Just three."
Mom:	"No way. That's too many."
Teen:	"How about two then?"
Mom:	"Well okay. But you have to stay downstairs [in their lovely recreation room] because we have company."

Incredibly, the mom actually thought she had won this discussion because she had talked her son down to just two friends. *Grounded* should mean no social activity, not that only two friends are allowed. The mother might have been influenced by not looking mean in front of her friends, but the result was that whatever the son had been grounded for received no real consequence at all. It is better not to use this consequence because it is too difficult for most parents to administer and it is not immediate enough. ——————————————————————

In summary, the main points about administering consequences are:

- Just do something. Don't worry about whether it is appropriate or not.
- Keep anger out of the situation.
- Impose the consequences immediately.
- Set a time limit.
- Don't make the consequences last too long. A few days at the most.
- Avoid grounding, unless the circumstances are extreme.

Unique Stepparenting Issues

As mentioned in the chapter introduction, the main aspect of the stepparenting situation that is different from discipline in a standard family is that the bond between the children and the new parent is not naturally present. This means that, unless it is done well, the discipline will be resented and the gulf between stepparent and stepchildren that is usually initially present will widen. This is when you will hear the infamous phrase "You're not my real parent. You can't tell me what to do." It is vital then that the stepparent follow all the above guidelines to administer the rules. That sounds simple, but for some reason, most stepparents simply are not aware of the guidelines and proceed to make elementary disciplining errors that lead to frustration for everyone.

Usually stepparents seem to expect that because the biological parent loves them, the kids will too. This is almost never the case. Most often the kids will reserve judgment until they see what this new person in their lives is like. In the worst-case scenario, they will be actively antagonistic, either because they don't want their unique relationship with their parent who is marrying to change or because they don't want to be disloyal to their other parent by liking this new one. Discipline can be the deal breaker if done poorly. All of a stepparent's positive acts will be dismissed as "sucking up" if that stepparent reacts angrily to the child's misbehaviours or if he or she is too tense and restrictive on a regular basis.

Another unique aspect of discipline for stepparents occurs when their mate has been single-parenting for a number of years. The children have gotten used to this parent's disciplining style, for better or worse, and cannot easily adjust to another disciplinary figure in their lives. This is especially true if the approaches to family regulation are radically different. The stepchildren are almost guaranteed to resent the influence of the new family member in this case. The solution is for the stepparent to try to observe the dynamics of family interaction for a while and attempt to have his or her style blend with that of the biological parent. If there is a radical difference in their disciplinary philosophies, it is vital that the parents sit down and discuss how to work together so that the children don't have to adjust to two different approaches. If they don't, the children will be unlikely to ever form a close relationship with their stepparent. The case of Fred and Mary provides an excellent example of what happens when the two parental disciplinary styles differ radically.

Mary had been on her own with her three children for almost six years before she met and rapidly married Fred. Most outside observers would have agreed that Mary's children were badly behaved. They were often rude to her; they came and went at their own discretion; and they refused to do household chores. They were not bad children, in that they did not get into trouble at school or with the law, but they were used to a very permissive system when in the home. Fred was extremely frustrated with the way the children treated their mother. He had been raised in a strict but loving home where such rude and cavalier behaviour was not accepted. He immediately started to correct this behaviour and was met with resistance from the two older children and, surprisingly, from Mary as well.

Mary had been concerned from the time of her divorce about the effects the breakup might have on the children and so was afraid that being firm with them would make the situation worse.

Although this was far from the truth, she had taken this permissive approach with them for the past few years and they had become used to it. Whenever Fred tried to discipline her children she would intervene on their behalf. Fred quickly felt isolated both from the children and, gradually, from Mary, too. He knew his approach to family discipline would be more effective but was powerless to change anything in the face of so much opposition. As a result, Fred and Mary began to argue frequently and, seeing the marriage to be in jeopardy, they sought the help of a counsellor.

The suggested approach was for the couple to sit down with the children and explain what had happened, what their concerns

were, and to seek solutions as a group to remedy the situation. The
result was an excellent meeting in which even the children agreed
that there should be a general tightening of the rules to eliminate
some of the inappropriate behaviours. It took a few weeks, but
gradually peace descended on the household as both parents
worked to blend their disciplinary system.

Rather than waiting for a crisis, this family meeting should have taken place right at the beginning of the marriage. Children, especially teenagers, can be very mature when adults give them the chance. As has been said earlier, children prefer discipline, but they can't handle sudden changes and a diversity of approaches. When this occurs, they will rebel and naturally tend to side with their biological parent.

An even more effective approach would be to anticipate the potential problem before the marriage ever takes place. Parents and prospective stepparents need to be aware of the danger represented by opposing disciplinary philosophies. The two adults should discuss the concept of discipline as soon as they realize that their relationship is serious. Once the prospective stepparent meets the kids a few times, he or she should already have an idea about what the discipline is like in the home. If a disparity in approach is noted, then a discussion needs to take place between them try to find a common approach. The problem has traditionally been that most parents and prospective stepparents do not realize how serious this issue is. In the glow of their love they tend to overlook this topic, often until it is too late. Since compromise is such an important part of any marriage, finding the middle ground with disciplinary approaches is a good place to start.

Another situation unique to stepfamilies occurs when the biological parent opts out of the discipline side of the marriage, leaving it to the stepparent. This was discussed in the previous chapter but is mentioned again here because this situation is so hard on a stepparent. Not only do they have full responsibility for the discipline of someone else's children, but the children can come to resent their own parent's lack of involvement. Their anger is then often directed at the stepparent, because that is safer than attacking their own parent's behaviour. This becomes very confusing to the stepparent, who knows that she is doing a good job but is still meeting considerable resistance from the stepchildren.

One tendency may be for the stepparent to back out of the process entirely and leave it to the natural parent. This approach might work when the biological mom or dad is at home, but will leave the stepparent helpless when he or she is left alone with the children. If some semblance of authority is not established at the very beginning of the relationship, it will be unlikely to develop at a later date. Teachers often find this out the hard way. If they don't establish control of their classrooms in September, they will have great difficulty gaining control in December. Stepparents are figuratively stepping into the raising of these children in December and are already behind in the disciplinary process. They can definitely get into a position of authority when necessary; it will just be much more difficult than it would be with their own children.

Discipline can definitely be a marriage wrecker for all marriages, but without that biological bond, stepparents are at a definite disadvantage. There must be a common approach to discipline in the family that is firm but fair. Above all, discipline must be delivered calmly. If stepparents follow the suggestions given in this chapter, their chances of success both with their inherited children and in their marriages will be greatly enhanced.

Blended Families

One of the major contentions of this book has been that stepparenting is far more difficult than most people realize, but that if care and effort are taken with the process, it can be accomplished successfully. This is also the case with blending families, which is a special circumstance of stepparenting; however, the difference is that even more care and effort are necessary with this blending process, since both parents will now be stepparents. Many more complications are present when blending families than exist for the simpler (but still difficult) stepparenting. The famous television show *The Brady Bunch* did a great disservice to all potential blended families by making the process look simpler than it really is. Certainly the Bradys encountered problems, but they were all relatively minor and all were solved in a half-hour. This will definitely not be the case in reality. It is entirely possible to blend families, but the adults entering this marriage have to realize that it is a complicated and difficult process, and that they will have to work hard to make the blending a success.

To understand what makes this blending process so difficult, it is helpful to review the complexities of regular stepparenting. In this case, there is a biological parent and a stepparent in the household. As a result of the emotions aroused in the children by the divorce, such as loyalty to the non-custodial parent and having lived with just one parent for a period of time, the new person in the household is often resented. When these emotions are compounded by the strangeness of having a new person in the house and differences in parenting styles between the natural parent and the stepparent, the resentment often grows, frequently resulting in open defiance to the new parent.

In a blended family the complexities of stepparenting are initially doubled. Both parents are now stepparents with all the challenges that this situation brings. However, there are also some added challenges, centring on the blending of the children. They all have different personalities and different emotional needs. Parents seem to expect that the kids will all be friends, despite their differences in personality and upbringing. This is simply not the case. While it can certainly happen that the children become instant friends, this is rare and should not be expected. There is no emotional bond between these children, as there is with natural brothers and sisters; their only connection is that their respective parents love each other. Unfortunately, this is rarely enough for the children to blend without difficulties. As a result, the parenting complexities as compared to normal stepparenting are considerably more—more than double. The purpose of this chapter is to examine these added complexities and propose solutions that will ease the blending process. If parents are aware of the possible problems before they enter matrimony, then most of them can either be avoided completely or resolved in a reasonable time period.

THE COMPLEXITY OF BLENDED FAMILIES

1. A traditional family of four, with parents who have two of their own children, has six relationships. They are:

   - mother with father
   - mother with child 1
   - mother with child 2
   - father with child 1
   - father with child 2
   - child 1 with child 2

2. A small blended family of four, where each child has a parent from a previous marriage, has 15 relationships. This increased complexity occurs because each parent also has an ex-spouse.

3. In cases where all of the divorced parents remarry someone who also had one child from a previous marriage, you now each have to navigate 44 relationships. If there is normal visitation with the ex-spouses, the two children in your particular blended family have to obey six different adults with differing ideas about discipline. They each have to learn to relate to children from three other families. All this complexity, and yet your family is only two adults and two kids.

4. Without doing the math, you can see that if each parent brings two children into a blended family, the number of relationships becomes staggering. ⸺⸺⸺⸺⸺⸺⸺

Blending the Parents

Several areas of parenting blended families are different from any other form of parenting and have the potential to cause problems in the marriage. Each of these areas first requires awareness that a problem might exist, and then a plan is necessary to combat the potential negative effects on family life before they become serious enough to threaten the marriage.

- **Family Organization**

  One of the easier potential problem areas to plan for is the increased organization that is necessary in most blended families. This organization is partly necessary because blended families tend to have more children in them than the average North American family (which currently stands at 1.8 children per family). The smallest possible blended family has two children, while most have three or four. In today's active, fast-paced world, children tend to be involved in many extracurricular activities and often both parents are working. While 2001 statistics indicate that about 56 percent of families have both parents working, this figure is probably higher in blended families, as both parents were likely working during their single-parenting days and often tend to continue working after their remarriage. The combination of children's activities and parents working means that when the parents get home, they will not be able simply to relax after a hard day's work. Instead, the chauffeuring to and from activities begins, with supper somehow having to be worked in. If parents in blended family situations are to stay sane, they will have to be extremely well-organized.

  Another reason for the increased chaos in blended families is visitation with the other biological parents. Blended families are more complex because both sets of children must make their prescribed visitations at various intervals. It would be ideal if both sets of kids were at their other parent's home on the same weekends and holidays, but this is rarely the case. These visitations often involve driving the kids

SCOTT WOODING

to their mother or dad's place and waiting for them to be returned at the end of the visitation period. This takes a huge amount of time and must be considered whenever family scheduling is being done.

The answer to the potential chaos of blended families lies in weekly scheduling. The first step is to obtain a large calendar with boxes for each day big enough to mark in all the daily activities for the week. A normal calendar sent out by the local bank or real estate agent will not do. If a commercial version does not exist, then families can make them up themselves and have them duplicated at one of the many public facilities that do custom photocopying. This calendar should be posted in a central location in the house and the children should be trained to check it frequently.

The next step is to have one of the parents designated to update the calendar each week. This is usually done most effectively on Sunday night. It doesn't really matter which parent does this chore, but usually one parent is more organized than the other, so the left-brained organizer type should do it. Another suggestion might be to have a second, longer-range calendar in the same area to mark down activities that are more than a week in the future. These dates can then be transferred each Sunday to the weekly chart.

Finally, along with these activity postings, weekly chore assignments can be listed. In more complex blended families with three or four children, one of the children might be designated to start the supper each night, one to do the cleanup or one to cut the lawn in the summer. Regular chores, such as room-cleaning or vacuuming need not be listed after the children have all learned these regular assignments. Only those jobs that change each week need be on the main calendar.

Along with the weekly calendar postings, a great time-saving device is to set up the daily meals ahead of time. This could be as simple as designating what each supper will be, or it could be as complex as actually cooking meals on the weekend and freezing them for use during the week. Either way, each night's menu can be put on the calendar for easy reference. Instructions as to where everything can be found also need to be given if the children are going to be responsible for any part of the meal preparation. They do have a tendency to forget things, and if the instructions are not clear, then you can expect your cell phone to be ringing at about 5:00 PM every day.

FAMILY DINNERS

In these complex times, the family dinner has become almost extinct. This is very sad because dinnertime has traditionally been the best time for family communication. Communication with kids happens most when everyone is relaxed, and supper times are usually relatively relaxed occasions. It is a time when parents can catch up on what's been happening in their children's lives. This communication time is even more important for blended families. It is not only good for finding out what's happening, but also as a time for the family to bond as a unit. Family dinners should not be ignored as a luxury. For newly blended families in particular, they should be considered mandatory.

• **Parenting Expectations**

A number of expectations about parenting held by some people can cause major difficulties in a blended family. One of these is that the wives are often expected to do the majority of the parenting. This is a leftover from pre-feminist times and can be a major strain for the female in a newly blended family, as she takes the brunt of trying to meld children from different backgrounds into one family unit. Fathers need to be heavily involved in the parenting process, if only because some of the kids are theirs. The complexity of combining what were two separate families into one unit requires the attention of two parents on an almost full-time basis. It is unfair and inconsiderate to leave the majority of parenting to the female of the relationship just because historically women have been the nurturers.

Another major expectation is that you will all instantly become one big happy family and that parenting will be just the same as it would be in a standard family with two natural parents. Nothing could be further from the truth. Instead, because of the biological ties between each parent and their children, as well as the history of interaction between the parents and their own children, the family commonly ends up as two mini-families, with each parent tending to look after problems involving their own children. In many cases, the parents even end up mainly interacting with their own children, so that the father attends his children's events and the mother goes to hers. The dad might take his children to the show while the mom goes to the amusement park with hers. Discipline in these situations can be different for dad's children than it is for mom's. This is a potentially explosive situation because the kids very quickly realize that there are different standards in the family

This mini-family situation often arises because it is easier to do things with children you know and have emotional ties with than it is to deal with children who are not your own. The solution lies in what could be termed *cross-parenting* where each parent tries to find ways to spend some time with the other parent's children. For example, the stepfather could take the mom's children to register for soccer, or mom could take the dad's kids to the recreation centre for swimming. The idea is to find opportunities to interact with and support the spouse's children so that you can get to know each other, and so that your spouse's children realize that you support them as much as you support your own kids.

Naturally, this cross-parenting should include attending the step-children's events along with their biological parent. Nothing shows your interest and appreciation for your stepchildren better than religiously attending all their games, recitals, and parent-teacher interviews. It is relatively painless, takes only a little time, and yet it is highly appreciated.

The idea is to try to treat all the children as your own. This simple concept is easier said than done. That emotional bond with your own children is very strong and many parents are insecure around other people's kids. If you are not naturally comfortable with children other than your own, it takes tremendous effort to treat them all equally. Often stepparents expect the children to adapt to them without the adult having to do anything special. This is unlikely to happen because they are just children. They lack the experience and maturity that adults should have, and they respond to novel situations with fear and apprehension, and their attendant emotions, such as anger or withdrawal. This means that it is up to the adults to do their utmost to make a connection with their spouse's children. It's not hard as long as it is not expected that this connection will happen immediately. Just attending a few events or taking the kids for ice cream a few times will not be enough. A full connection will take years, but when the stepchildren realize that you are trying, you will get through the testing period described in Chapter 4 fairly quickly and reach a stage of truce. The harder the adult tries to relax and have fun with the stepchildren, the quicker the painful adaptation process goes and the sooner a true family situation can develop.

One of the impediments that will slow this family development process will usually be the tactics employed by the children to get their way in disputed situations. Most of these were described in Chapter 4 in the discussion of the Testing Phase, but there is one tactic that is particularly found in blended family situations. This is the divide-and-conquer technique. Parents need to be aware of the tendency for children to try to get what they want, either by going to their own parent when their stepparent is the stricter one, relying on that emotional bond to get their own way, or by approaching the stepparent, knowing that he or she is not familiar with their previous family rules. This is a natural tendency employed frequently in "normal" families, but it is much easier to use in blended situations.

It is important to realize that this tactic is not the result of covert planning on the children's part but occurs to them by instinct. Kids want what they want when they want it and will do whatever they can to get it. Stepparents should not resent or get angry with this tactic, but need to be aware of it in order to provide a united front when their kids attempt to divide and conquer. The tendency when the spouse's children employ this tactic is to think that his or her kids are sneaky and underhanded and get angry with them. This attitude will interfere with the bonding process. A more effective technique is simply to call the kids on it, with some humour if possible, to show that you understand what they are doing and will not be fooled by it—but you don't blame them for trying.

- **Parenting Mine, Yours, and Ours**

One of the most frustrating aspects of parenting in blended families is trying to cope with the children's perceptions. No matter how hard you try to be fair and equitable to all the children, no matter whose they are, the kids will see discrepancies in how they are treated. In many cases, of course, they will be right. Parents do have a natural tendency to accept more from their own children than they will from other people. However, it is particularly galling to be accused of favouring your own children when you are certain you're not doing so.

There are several reasons for the development of this situation. Kids discover that accusations of favouritism can be a particularly good method of getting their own way. Again, this appears to be an instinctive technique rather than a planned strategy, but it works because they are playing on stepparental guilt feelings; the non-biological parent is empathetic to what his or her stepchildren are going through and perhaps feels a little sorry for them. This causes the stepparent to try too hard not to upset them, so when they get accused of favouritism toward their own children, they give in.

Another reason for stepchildren's accusations of favouritism with little or no justification is that they expect their new parents to like their own children better. The children will often see unfairness when it does not exist because they fully believe that it will happen. It seems only natural to them that parents would protect their own children over stepchildren, so they often "see" it happening when it really isn't. This is particularly frustrating for stepparents who are trying very hard to be fair, yet get accused of favouritism anyway. Many stepparents get so frustrated that they quit trying; after all, why bother working to be fair when your efforts are not appreciated? Unfortunately, while understandable, this attitude will not help the situation. Instead, sitting down and discussing perceived unfairness with the stepchild often goes a long way toward solving the situation and preventing future problems. The best forum for this is often the family meeting. These were discussed earlier, but they should be mandatory for all blended families on at least a biweekly basis.

Finally, many stepchildren cry unfairness and inequity as a sign of their anger and frustration with their life situation. If they weren't ready for their parent to marry because they had still not worked through their breakup baggage, or if they were unhappy with the parent's choice of a mate, crying foul may be the stepchild's way of trying to communicate his or her frustration. This may also be a more bitter form of the divide-and-conquer technique, where the motive, whether conscious or subconscious, is actually to divide the marriage. In this case, hard work by both parents is necessary to resolve the underlying anger, and, more than likely, counselling will be necessary.

Jody, a 15-year-old grade 10 student, was taken to a counsellor because her marks were very poor. She complained that she didn't like her fellow classmates or the teachers, and it seemed to the counsellor that the best approach was to change schools. This was done and it worked for the rest of the school year. Early the next year, Jody came back to the counsellor, at her request. This time the problem was that her stepfather was treating her unfairly.

SCOTT WOODING

According to Jody, he often let his own children stay out past curfew with no sanctions, but if she were just five minutes late she would be grounded. When this perceived unfairness was discussed with her stepfather, he was stunned. He felt that he had been working hard for the past three years to be fair to all four children and had no idea Jody thought he was favouring his own children. Further conversation with Jody uncovered a very deep-rooted anger about her mother's remarrying. It was the real reason that her marks had dropped at her initial school, and this anger was also causing her to see unfairness in her stepfather's actions where it really didn't exist.

Jody had never accepted her parents' breakup and had hoped they would get back together. She was totally unprepared for her mother to remarry and had only been vaguely aware that she was dating someone. Jody did not realize it, but subconsciously she felt that it would be unacceptable to be angry with her mother. As a result, she tried to bring attention to her feelings first by doing poorly in school and later by blaming her stepfather. Since all these tactics were subconsciously motivated, it took many sessions to help her to realize the cause of her anger and to express it in a more realistic way. The counselling also included the mother and stepfather, who instituted family meetings to allow a more appropriate setting for discussing such concerns.

- **Alone Time**

The chaos of parenting in a blended family situation leaves very little time for the parents to be together alone. Alone time is necessary to maintain the marriage, as it allows time for communication important to adults. This may be as mundane as the happenings in each other's workplace or it may be a chance to discuss issues that arise in their marriage or parenting. For communication to take place, there must first be time for it to do so and then there must be a setting conducive to conversation. This setting is rarely the home because there are always little ears present to overhear and possibly misinterpret conversations, and there are frequent interruptions from the children, the phone, and the doorbell.

Wise parents in any marriage will allow time to keep their marriage strong. Not only should they be using this alone time for communication, they need to be having some fun together as well. Bowling, movies, concerts, working out, or just having coffee together in a favourite café are all ways to have fun and to converse. There is no need to feel guilty about leaving the kids with a sitter once in a while. If the marriage doesn't stay strong—or worse, doesn't survive—the kids will suffer far more than they ever would from their parents' being absent for a few hours. A weekly or biweekly "date night" should be pencilled into the family calendar and then held sacred as a vital component of a sound marriage.

• Family Traditions

A key element that gets lost in a divorce is the family's traditions. These are often built around holidays, especially the major ones like Christmas and Easter. Maybe the whole family gathered at Grandma and Grandpa's house for the turkey dinner at Christmas each year, or everyone participated in an Easter egg hunt at Aunt Mary's every Easter Sunday. These traditions help to give a family its character and identity, but their importance to the children is often underrated by adults. When a divorce occurs, these traditions automatically stop and leave a void in the children's lives.

It only stands to reason that if traditions help to define a family and give it its character, then it would be wise for newly minted blended families to institute some. These can be decided on as a group if the children are old enough, so that when the first Christmas together is approaching, everyone can sit down and decide on what activities and rituals can be set for the coming holiday season. Similar meetings can be held for other major holidays, including summer vacations. In fact, one of the traditions can be the family meeting held in February or March to determine where the family will go on holiday this year.

If the children are too young for this process, then the adults can decide on some appropriate traditions to set to begin with, and then gradually allow family participation as the children get older. The key element in this process is that traditions should be inviolate. They should be set in such as way that they can be repeated each year without interruption or they will never be "traditional." As the children move into their teen years, they will often find other activities, usually with friends, that they want to do instead of following family tradition. This should never be allowed. A family tradition needs to be forever, so that as the family grows and eventually expands, new people, such as spouses and children, can benefit from the traditions as well. Parents have to resist any exceptions unless there are life-threatening circumstances, or the tradition will very soon not exist.

These traditions are essential to the development of a strong family feeling and should occupy an important part of each family's lifestyle.

- **Positive Teamwork**

As was discussed in great detail in Chapter 1, divorces tend to result in a plethora of strong emotions that can not only interfere with a remarriage but can virtually destroy it. One of the phenomena of remarriage is that a new spouse will often adopt the battle being waged between the new partner and his or her ex, and enthusiastically join the fight. In this circumstance, the spouse may "help" by thinking up new ways to get back at the new partner's ex. This may seem like support, but the fact is that this could actually contribute to the demise of the remarriage by encouraging the breakup baggage not only to continue but to escalate. This adds to the stress of the family rather than decreasing it by letting the baggage go. This could be considered negative teamwork.

Collateral damage is also caused by this tactic because it will clearly affect the children. If they are caught in the middle of a battle between their mother and father, aided and abetted by their stepparent, the kids are bound to suffer emotionally, as they will be under pressure from both parental sides to join their respective causes. Kids can't do this in most cases because they love both parents. The result is increased stress on the children, which will cause them to react emotionally, such as by acting out or by doing poorly in school. This in turn puts more pressure on the adults and on their marriage.

A more effective strategy would be for the partners in these blended situations to provide more positive support by helping each other to recover from any breakup baggage that might still exist rather than by pitching in to encourage it. This may not be as easy as it sounds. Parents who have been fighting these divorce battles, either for changes to custody arrangements or for more child support (or perhaps even *any* child support) are usually heavily committed emotionally to the battle and may resent any attempts to mollify them. Still, it is important to end the fighting, and, as an outside person, a new spouse can have a much more objective viewpoint and needs to actively try to convey it to their battling spouse. The uninvolved spouse can also advocate support groups or counselling help in order to affect this positive teamwork that is so much more effective in developing a close family. Working together to rid the family of breakup baggage will pay huge dividends in family harmony.

Joan had been divorced for three years and had primary custody of the two children. She would be classed as one of the "working poor" because her wages barely covered her expenses each month. Money for any so-called extras, such as clothing or school supplies for the children, had to come from her ex-husband. He had remarried to a woman with two children of her own. He paid little child support and what he did pay had to be forced on him by the court. This puzzled Joan because her husband appeared to genuinely love his kids, and she did not understand why he was so reluctant to support them. Joan hated asking him for money because of the negative reaction she always got, but if their kids were to have even the bare necessities, she had no other choice.

The facts of the situation were clearly brought home to her one day when she asked her husband for money to take their eight-year-old son to a counsellor. The school had noticed some serious emotional problems in the lad and had recommended counselling. Her husband appeared to be listening to her at first but suddenly she could hear his wife yelling, "Don't give that bitch a cent." She had been listening on the extension and now actively entered the conversation, telling Joan that she should get a better job and quit pestering her ex-husband for money all the time now that he had a new family to support. She also told Joan that her ex-husband was weak and that she was the strong one and there was no way she would get any more money from them.

It was obvious that her ex's reluctance to pay for anything was at least partially being fuelled by his new wife's extreme reactions. This was hurting the children in many ways, but to refuse money for his son to get the help he needed was just plain mean. This kind of negative teamwork never solves any disputes. In fact, it almost inevitably makes them become more intense and longer lasting. Ultimately it could also cause friction between Joan's ex-husband and his new wife, as he would probably learn to stand up for himself eventually, for the sake of his kids, and begin to defy her.

The ultimate nightmare scenario exists when both parents in a blended family are dealing with hostile ex-spouses. The tension that this unfortunate circumstance creates can be unbearable. There is no easy answer for this situation, but the solution is still the same. Both participants in the marriage have to support each other in a positive way by helping each other not to retaliate against the former spouses and to refrain from sinking to their level. This is truly asking for sainthood, but nothing else will work. Responding in kind to the hostility and resorting to similar shady tactics will only prolong the battle. Seeking support from the courts is extremely expensive and, even if you win, these judgements are difficult to enforce. The only effective answer is to support each other in ignoring the antagonism from the exes and get on with your own lives.

Blending the Children

As mentioned in the introduction to this chapter, blending children from two different family backgrounds is not easy. Unfortunately, most parents in blended situations do not seem to realize this when they decide to get married. They may be vaguely aware that stepparenting is not easy; however, they seem to miss the concept that all children are not instantly compatible. It would be nice if, seeing that their parents are happy in their new relationship, the children would try extra hard to make the situation work. They won't! Children rarely have the maturity to make this kind of resolution and, even if they do, they do not have the emotional wisdom to follow such a resolution through. Parents must take the children's needs and feelings into consideration before the marriage happens and then make frequent adjustments after the fact. Blending the children is an aspect that makes the process of blending families much more difficult than stepparenting alone.

A) Readiness Problems

One of the great injustices of this world is that all children do not have the same personality characteristics. While a person might argue, with considerable justification, that no one would want all kids to be the same, it would certainly make parenting easier. It would be much simpler to practice parenting on the first child so that you could get it right for any subsequent children. The fact is, though, that all children are different and this is particularly true when it comes to emotions. Some children are more sensitive than others and have greater needs for overt signs of love and for emotional stability. In a divorce this means that some children will adapt to the situation faster than others and will, therefore, be more accepting of a remarriage than their sibling might be.

Parents in blended situations should be aware of the feelings of their children to a remarriage, preferably before the marriage occurs. Some children will be happy that their parents are remarrying, others will be conflicted, understanding why their mother or father wants to remarry but not quite sure about it, while many children will be dead set against the marriage. Parents *must* have many open discussions with their children before the marriage to determine at what stage their children might be with their feelings. Parents should not just assume that a child opposed to a remarriage will "come around." They might eventually, but for several years everyone's life will be miserable, especially the stepparent's. If one or more of the children isn't ready, then it is not a good idea for the marriage to happen.

If all the steps of Chapter 2 have been followed in the courtship process, then most kids will be ready for the nuptials. Unfortunately, many people won't reach for a book such as this one for help until they are well into the problem. There just isn't enough common information passed around about this subject for parents to prevent problems from occurring in blended family situations. On the contrary, shows like *The Brady Bunch* and movies such as *Yours, Mine and Ours* have generated the myth that blending families is a relatively easy process with just a few wrinkles. As a result, many blended families find themselves with one or more unhappy children.

If this situation occurs, it can be remedied, but it will take time. The remedy is in three parts. The first is effective communication between the biological parent and the recalcitrant child. It will serve no purpose to get angry with the child for his or her feelings. The kids are too young to be able to rationalize or understand them. If this is puzzling to a parent, think about how childish adults can be in a divorce—and they should be old enough to know better. Children will not be able to just "get over it," instead they need an adult with whom they can discuss their feelings. The biological parent is the natural outlet.

The secret to this communication is in being able to listen uncritically to the child's concerns. The tendency for most adults is to become defensive or to minimize the concerns expressed. This will result in an instant blockage of communication and the child's worries will not be expressed. Instead, try to draw out the feelings by asking questions about whatever is expressed instead of making excuses or replying with clichés. Here are a few examples of how communication gets blocked by defensiveness and minimization:

> *Mom:*   *"Why are you always so rude to Jim (stepfather)?"*
>
> *Sue:*   *"I hate him."*
>
> *Mom:*   *"Oh, you don't really hate him. Give him some time and once you know him better you'll like him."*

This discourse minimizes Sue's feelings. The mother is actually denying that Sue feels this way. Mom may be right that her daughter doesn't really "hate" her new stepfather, but she certainly does not like him, and denying that these feelings exist will instantly shut down the communication. Here's another example of how not to communicate:

> *Mom:*   *"Why won't you do anything that Jim asks you to do?"*
>
> *Sue:*   *"I don't like him telling me what to do."*
>
> *Mom:*   *"Well, I love him and I think that for my sake you should be nicer to him."*

That's a defensive reaction and it puts a bit of a guilt trip on the child. That's not only unfair, but it is guaranteed to get a defensive reaction in return, and an argument is almost certainly going to result. Instead, the conversation should go as follows:

Mom:	*"How come you spend so much time in your room when Jim is around?"*
Sue:	*"Because I don't like him. He creeps me out."*
Mom:	*"Oh, really? How does he do that?"*
Sue:	*"He's always talking to me like I was a little kid. And I hate it when he hangs all over you. Why did you have to marry him anyway?" (Here the real problem starts to come out.)*
Mom:	*"Well, I really love him. What do you think we can do to make things better?"*
Sue:	*"I don't know. Maybe he could start talking to me as if I was a real person instead of always talking down to me."*
Mom:	*"Can you give me some examples?"*

By continually asking for Sue's input and ideas, Mom can keep the conversation flowing, extract information, and come up with some solutions. The next step will be to convince Jim to participate in addressing Sue's concerns. This time it is the stepdad who will have to avoid being defensive. Most of the time he would not be trying to offend Sue, but just did not realize that she was upset. Many of the concerns are actually minor ones. The problem really was that Sue was not ready for her mother's remarriage. One excellent technique in this communication process is to ask for Sue's ideas as to what they can do to resolve her concerns. Kids, especially teens, often have excellent ideas and they feel validated when the ideas are listened to and occasionally accepted.

The second step in dealing with children who are not accepting the remarriage well is to get the stepparent actively involved. This is the cross-parenting concept that was mentioned earlier. To get a child to participate in activities with a stepparent he or she does not like may be difficult, but patience and persistence will win out eventually. The trick for the stepparent is to be able to be patient and to keep asking the child to go places and do things with him or her. Many stepparents are stunned when their partner's child rebuffs them and responds with defensiveness and anger. Statements like, "What's the matter with that son of yours? You need to teach him better manners," are often made. These not only do not take into account the natural feelings of the child but also put the biological parent on the defensive. This parent feels caught in the middle and often will defend his or her child, resulting in an argument. There is nothing wrong with the youngster; it is the adult who needs to recognize the problem and respond with patience and kindness—even in the face of rudeness and defiance. This is certainly difficult to do. It's like turning the biblical "other cheek." Still, a continued expression of interest in the child's activities, frequently asking the young person on an outing and exhibiting patience and under-standing in the face of the child's negative emotions will win in the end.

Finally, it is vital that family meetings be a regular event when one or more children is not responding well to the remarriage. To this point, fam-ily meetings have been a strong suggestion for all blended families. When a child shows that he or she was not ready for the marriage, then they should be mandatory on a weekly basis.

REMEDIES WHEN A CHILD RESPONDS POORLY TO REMARRIAGE

- Good communication with the biological parent.
- Listening and questioning techniques are vital.
- Patient and persistent cross-parenting attempts by the stepparent.
- Regular family meetings on a weekly basis. ——————————

B) Competition for Parental Attention

Once a family is blended by the addition of a stepparent's children, each biological parent will find that they no longer have as much time to spend with their own children as they did before the remarriage. They have lunches to make for the extra kids, places to drive the stepchildren and events of theirs to attend. In many such cases, parents will find that their children notice this difference in attention and often resent it. This is especially true if there had been a prolonged period of single-parenting before the marriage. When this resentment occurs, children will often start to employ techniques to get their parent's undivided attention. These techniques include only inviting their own parent to parent-teacher interviews, recitals, and games. They also include asking their biological parent to take them places, like shopping or to the movies, in an attempt to keep their mother or father to themselves.

While this tendency is natural, it cannot be allowed to occur too frequently. There may be times when the children have their parent to themselves, such as a trip to their grandparent's place, but the majority of the time it will be necessary to insist that the stepparent and/or his or her children also be present. This will cultivate the idea that this is now one family and all children and parents will be treated the same. Allowing the children to split the group up into mini-families will be self-defeating and cannot be allowed.

Having said this, *how* things are done is once again just as important as *what* is done. In this case, it is understandable that the children would want to be alone with their parent, so there is no need to get angry with them. Instead, the insistence on family togetherness should be done with patience and understanding. The reasons may need to be explained many times by both parents to their own children, or by both parents to all the children but, if done calmly, the message will eventually be received and even accepted.

C) Same-aged Children

One of the major fallacies that exists in newly blended families is that children of the same age and sex will have the same interests and friends. As a result, they will end up friends with each other. This may indeed happen, but it cannot be anything but an ideal. If it occurs, great, but chances are it will not. Parents, both biological and step, must allow room for differences and not expect children of the same age to have the same abilities and interests or to hang around together. In fact, being the same age may make them bitter rivals, especially when it comes to friends of both the same and opposite sexes.

Children of the same age may be rivals in many areas of their lives. One of the most potentially damaging comparisons can be in the academic area. Parents in normal families often make the mistake of comparing the academic abilities of their children. If the first is very bright in school, they may have difficulty accepting the fact that the next child is not. It is even more tempting to do this in a blended family with children of the same age. The fact is that the children are highly unlikely to have the same academic abilities or even the same work habits. Comparisons between these children are not only unfair, but they can be very harmful to the child who has the lesser ability. This can cause resentment to smoulder toward the parents and often to the stepsibling as well. This is not the atmosphere parents want to develop in their blended family.

This same situation occurs with athletic ability, musical aptitude, or even in clothing and musical tastes. It is a huge bonus when the kids can share clothes and DVDs, go to the same lessons, or play on the same teams. Unfortunately, this rarely occurs. Different children, even those of the same age and sex, are different, and this needs to be clearly recognized and supported by both parents. Suggestions such as, "Why don't you two go to a movie tonight?" or "Baseball tryouts are in a week. Why don't you both try out for the Hawks?" will often be inflammatory and lead to someone's having hurt feelings or resenting you or their stepsibling. Conversations between the two parents, preferably before marriage, can elicit the strengths and interests of each child. These should be scanned for similarities and, if there are any, then encouragement in those areas is logical. However, if few common areas of ability or interest are found, parents must recognize this and allow the same-aged children to go their own ways at their own pace.

One of the trickiest areas to deal with for same-age, same-sex kids is that of friends. If both children are outgoing, make friends easily, and have similar interests, there will rarely be a problem. Each child will have his or her own friends and all will be well. The problems start when one child has a group of friends and the other does not. This friendless state may be because the child is quieter and less outgoing, or it may be because this child has moved into a home in an area different from where he or she had lived and does not yet know anyone. These children may have the tendency to try to "piggyback" on their stepsibling's friends. In other words, this child may try to hang out with the same kids, despite the fact that they are friends of their stepsibling. This situation can cause a tremendous amount of resentment and rivalry from the child who "owns" the friends.

The solution for the parents lies in patience and negotiation. The first step is to sit down with both kids, perhaps in a family meeting, and get the problem out in the open. Each child should be allowed to state his or her case and then arbitration needs to occur. If there are good reasons for the youngsters to share the friends, then ways to do this need to be negotiated. One useful approach is to try to find out what the other kids in the group think. This can be done by calling their parents. If, on the other hand, it is determined that it is not a good idea to try to share the friends, then the parents need to find ways that the friendless child can make companions of his or her own. This will almost certainly involve finding activities that will allow the child to be exposed to a different group of kids. Since, in this case, the children's interests are probably different anyway, separate activities will allow the opportunity to develop their own friends.

The key is never to try to force the situation. Kids choose their friends on the basis of common interests and personalities, and someone who does not fit into this group, no matter that this person is the same age, cannot be shoved in. Just give the rejected one a chance to find friends of his or her own if the common-friends approach does not work.

D) Personal Space

One of the most unanticipated aspects of blending families is the friction that can result from poorly allocated personal space. Since blended families tend to be larger than the standard, and since the average house has three bedrooms, assigning bedrooms to the children can often be a problem.

When there are more than two children in the blended family, assumptions are often made about which children should share a room. For example, if there are two boys and one girl, it is only natural that the boys be housed together. Other plans might have the two children from one family together, regardless of sex if they are young, while the child of the other parent has the single room. While these assumptions may be logical, they often do not take personalities into account. In fact, it is not wise for parents of blended families to make assumptions; a better idea is to check with the kids.

Many factors could end up causing friction and jealousies among the children as a result of bedroom assignments. Suppose two teenage girls are billeted together because of the age similarity, and one turns out to be relatively untidy while the other is a neat freak. The conflict resulting from this situation may start with the room situation, but could easily escalate into a personal dislike of each other. This is no way to blend a family. Similarly, putting a brother and sister into the same room can lead to an increase in normal sibling rivalries because they are closer together physically than they would be if they had separate rooms. Also, as they get older, sexuality and personal hygiene issues enter the picture and complicate matters considerably.

While in many cases there may be no such problems at all, it is far better to exercise some prevention than to blithely assume all will be well. If the parents are wrong, the conflicts could seriously interfere with the family atmosphere that they are trying to create. A better plan is to discuss the situation in a family meeting before moving in together. This will give the kids a chance to express their concerns and to give their suggestions. It is often fascinating to find that children, especially teens, can come up with some excellent solutions to potential problems such as this one. Throw the issue out and then carefully listen to their input. Watch the body language to ensure that no child is giving in just to please the parents or to avoid conflict. If the meeting is done according to the outline given in an earlier chapter, then everyone's concerns will be aired and potential solutions can be found.

If this is not done, then problems may fester for months before exploding and, by the time this explosion does occur, personal animosities may have formed that go beyond the relatively simple problem that caused them. Remember that there are other factors at play that create difficulties for a blending family. These are the emotional issues that can take many years to resolve fully. Parents do not want family progress to be held back by a physical issue that can be solved by relatively simple expedients such as asking kids who they would like to room with or by building a room in the basement.

E) Chores

Another sleeper issue—one that parents do not expect to be a problem but which can sneak up on them—is that of family chores. Children can be very alert for fairness, and the assignment of chores is guaranteed to be focused on by children in a blended family. As we have seen, children expect that biological parents will favour their own children and, as a result, are especially watchful for any signs that this is occurring. If they feel that chores are being doled out unfairly, then watch for an angry response.

The important thing to realize about children is that they cannot easily voice the reason for their anger. They may be afraid to upset their parents; they may be too shy; or perhaps they are not sure themselves what the problem really is. Whatever the reason, their anger may be expressed indirectly rather than by their simply stating that they think they are being given an unfair proportion of the household tasks. For parents in blended family situations, aware that children expect unfairness to occur, it is easier to anticipate this problem than it is to try to discover the source of a child's anger at a later date.

Several situations can provoke cries of unfairness. Older children may feel that they have to do "everything" while their younger siblings do "nothing." Female family members may think that they have to do more than their male counterparts, while children of one parent may feel that their stepparent's children get all the breaks.

Once again, this is an issue that should be addressed before the family blends, and then readdressed periodically in family meetings. As children grow, they can accept more responsibilities, but often these are not assigned to them but simply left with the older child who has been carrying them. This provokes the battle cry of the teenager—"That's Not Fair!" Parents need to make a list of the chores that will be the responsibility of the children and then meet to discuss as fair an allocation as possible. Children realize that they should do chores; they are just not good at doing them. By allowing the children input into which chores they would prefer to do, then parcelling them out as fairly as possible, future problems can be prevented.

F) Money Issues

Money is an important issue for children. When asked why children are not receiving allowances, the answer in this relatively affluent day is, "When my kids need money, I give it to them." This may work much of the time, although it does not teach anything, but problems can appear when children from differing family backgrounds bring along with them diverse philosophies about money. Ex-spouses, aunts and uncles, and grandparents may give birthday, Christmas, and Easter presents in monetary rather than in a more tangible form. (This phenomenon is probably related to the fact that no one has time to shop anymore, and don't get me started on this one!) Those relations with generous natures or with larger bank balances donate liberally to the family's youngsters, while those who are more parsimonious or who are not as well off tend to give smaller amounts.

This situation can create fiscal imbalances within the blended family. The children of one parent may have far more ready cash than the kids of the other parent. This means that one group will have all the trappings of the modern teenager, such as computers, video games, mp3s, and DVDs, while the other children have considerably less. The potential for friction in this situation between the haves and the have nots is huge and should be avoided at all costs.

One answer lies in effective communication between the have parent and his or her relatives. These parents must explain the situation in the new family and ask for restraint on the relative's part. This can be a delicate situation because grandparents in particular love to spoil their grandkids. Ex-spouses, especially those still immersed in breakup baggage, will automatically resent being told how much to give their children. If it is not possible to convince some relatives to restrain the size of their largesse, then the answer is to restrain your children's spending. This can also be difficult, but children do understand fairness. When the situation is explained carefully and thoroughly to them, they will usually understand why the personal possessions of one group of children should match that of the other kids in the blended family. The surplus funds from the unrestrained giving can be saved for future education, which is always a good cause. Some of it could even be donated to charity—an excellent teaching tool for young children.

Money has been said to be the root of all evil, and even if that is an exaggeration, money can be a wedge that can very quickly separate children in a blended family situation into two mini-families. Parents need to be aware that this circumstance can become divisive and head the issue off at the pass.

THE IMPORTANCE OF ALLOWANCES

In this relatively affluent time, parents often do not believe that allowances are important. Since they can afford not only the basic needs for their children, but many luxuries as well, they seem to consider the allowance as an old custom dating back to the Great Depression. Nothing could be further from the truth. There are few teaching tools as useful as the allowance, and it should be a part of every family, blended or standard. The reasons for this are as follows:

- It teaches budgeting. By receiving a standard amount on a weekly basis, children learn that if they spend it all the first day, there is nothing left for the rest of the week. That is very similar to adult life where the paycheque has to last for the entire pay period.
- It teaches saving. If children want an item that the parents consider to be a luxury, they can save for it out of their allowance. For relatively expensive items, parents can make a deal to pay half if the child saves the other half, but the concept of saving for desired items is still ingrained in the child. Again, this is similar to the adult world.
- It teaches that money is a limited commodity. In adult life people do not hand out money just because you want it. While you are giving children the money in an allowance, it is a limited amount so children learn that it does not "grow on trees."
- It gives and teaches independence. Having money of their own reduces the feeling of dependence on the parents that having to ask for it gives. It also allows a child to make decisions about how the allowance should be spent. These aspects allow the development of independence. —————————

SCOTT WOODING

Blending families is much harder than any other aspect of marriage and parenting. It is important for parents contemplating remarriage to be aware of this. However, despite the difficulties, it is entirely possible to blend if the potential problems are recognized ahead of time and dealt with before they occur or as soon as they arise. Patience and persistence, along with the tools described in this chapter, are all that is necessary. Of these tools, the family meeting is without doubt the most important. These meetings are an absolutely essential feature of the great majority of successful blended families, and their importance should never be underestimated.

Chapter 7

Teenagers:
A Special Case

If stepparenting and blending families were not hard enough, putting teenagers into the mix adds one more complication to these already difficult tasks. It is common knowledge that teenagers are unlike younger children and that they can be more difficult to parent. The majority of parents in normal family situations fear the teenage years and generally grit their teeth during this period, hoping just to survive it, an attitude often expressed in such phrases as, "If you think he's difficult now, wait until he becomes a teenager."

The problem with such fearfulness is that it leads to overreaction to much of the teen's behaviour. Personalities do change during the teen years, bringing often frustrating behaviours; nonetheless, many parents seem to think that it won't happen to them. When it does, they get upset, believing that something is wrong with their parenting. They feel guilty and frustrated and often take their child's actions and attitudes personally, as if they were planned acts of aggression against them. As a result, they react angrily to behaviours that even the teenagers don't understand. In return, the teens get angry, and the situation deteriorates into a shouting match.

The tragedy is that none of this is necessary. Understanding why personalities change during the teenage years, bringing about inexplicable behavioural changes, allows us to take a different attitude to them, resulting in a calmer, more reasoned approach. This will now permit parents to deal with these behaviours more effectively, resulting in fewer blowups and a closer, friendlier family situation.

The problem in stepparenting situations is that the teenagers are not the stepparent's own. The biological bond that normally develops with our children when they are infants isn't there. That bond gives biological parents "ownership" of their children and usually allows them to tolerate more from them than they would from someone else's. The situation is particularly difficult for stepparents who come into the family when their partner's children are already teenagers. They are instantly presented with teenage behaviour from children not their own. They lack that biological bond with the children, and their unfamiliarity with youngsters in this age group causes them to be particularly upset by such things as rudeness, failure to do chores, and sleeping in until noon on weekends. Behaviours that might mildly upset a biological parent can enrage a stepparent. This can result in conflict between the biological parent and the stepparent, often to the point of ending the relationship.

Once again, the solution is for stepparents to understand the dynamics of teenage behaviour and learn to deal with it calmly and effectively rather than with anger and frustration. With teens, anger will almost always be met with anger as they quickly become defensive—even when they know they were in the wrong. This will cause what might have been a relatively minor situation to escalate to a major battle, often eliciting the stepchild's battle cry, "You're not my real parent ..." By handling the situation in a more relaxed manner, a stepparent can avoid these battles and forge a real relationship with their teenaged stepchild while still achieving the desired result.

SCOTT WOODING

Understanding Teenage Behaviour

There are two major components that drive teenage behaviour: one that parents have known about for years (but still have not fully understood) and one that has only been discovered through some very sophisticated research. An understanding of both components is necessary to understand what causes personalities to change as children move into adolescence.

The Hormones

For generations parents have understood, at least vaguely, that hormones play a major role in teenage development. They may say to each other, "It's just hormones," to explain some undesirable aspect of their child's behaviour. Unfortunately, they haven't really understood what this statement means. Parents understand that hormones, particularly the sex hormones such as testosterone in the males and estrogen in the females, are the main determinants of the physical changes of puberty. When the brain matures to a certain point, chemicals are released that result in the discharge of these hormones and the process of physical maturation begins. Parents know that their children's bodies are getting ready to produce children of their own; the girls will develop breasts and start their menstrual cycles, and boys will get deeper voices, start to get hair on their bodies, and have nocturnal emissions. While many parents may not like seeing their children growing up in this obvious way, they at least understand it.

What they don't understand is that along with these physiological changes there must be psychological changes as well. In order for adolescents to start families of their own, they must be able to make decisions for themselves and to function independently of their parents. This independence may not be as vital today as it was in previous generations because parents now live longer. Even a century ago, life spans were much shorter and it was necessary for children to become independent quickly because they would soon be on their own. Many of today's problems occur because of the clash between a teenager's growing need for independence and the parent's tendency to treat them like children. This need for independence on the part of teens is displayed in many ways, most of which tend to irritate their uninformed parents.

Perhaps the earliest psychological sign that children are entering adolescence is their tendency to argue. Suddenly your formerly complacent child is arguing even the most mundane statements. If you say, "It's a beautiful day today" (and it is), you may be met with "There's too many clouds." That kind of response puzzles and frustrates most parents because it seems very negative and unnecessary. What they don't realize is that the response has nothing to do with the weather. It is just a teenager's way of saying "Hey, look at me. I've got an opinion now, too." By offering opinions opposite to those of their parents, brothers and sisters, news commentators, and teachers, teenagers are simply showing signs of wanting to have their own ideas and opinions, separate from those of their elders. Often these opinions make no sense at all, while at other times they can be thoughtful and intelligent. It doesn't really matter to the teens. They just need to express their own opinions periodically to show that they are now different people from their parents and other elders.

The problem with teens arguing is that it upsets and annoys their parents (and often their teachers) who are used to being the source of all family wisdom. What tends to happen to parents faced with an obviously ludicrous statement like, "I think Saddam Hussein was a really good leader," is that they get drawn into arguments. Rather than realizing that the teen is just displaying early signs of independence and the ability to form his or her own opinions, the adult tends either to try to counter the statement with an opposite argument, or simply to say something like, "Don't be ridiculous." Both methods are doomed to failure. No matter how outrageous their opinions, teens will be forced to defend them if their views are negated or ridiculed. This will inevitably result in an argument that no one can win because it has no base in reality. The base is actually the teenager's need to be different from his or her parents. The standard sequence of events usually goes something like this:

SCOTT WOODING

Teen: *"There's no such thing as global warming."*

Parent: *"Of course there is. Don't be silly."*

Teen: *"You never listen to me. You always treat me like a kid."*

Parent: *"Well, that's what happens when you say dumb things."*

Teen: *"I am not dumb!"*

... and the battle is on.

A much more effective way of dealing with teenage opinions is to use a questioning technique to see what the origins of the opinion are. Parents need to stay calm, recognizing that the opinions and ideas expressed by their teenager are often based on their need to be different and to have their own ideas, and not on attention seeking or defiance. This questioning technique would go as follows:

Teen: *"There's no such thing as global warming."*

Parent: *"Oh? Why do you think that?"*

Teen: *"Because this summer has been so cold."*

Parent: *"Has it been this cold everywhere this summer?"*

Teen: *"I don't know."*

Parent: *"Let's look on the Internet to see what's been happening in the rest of the world."*

... and a real conversation has begun.

By taking any expressed opinion relatively seriously and probing into its origins, a discussion can occur without anger and frustration. Teens feel validated when their opinions are not immediately dismissed or negated and their need for independent thought is met. Not only that, but a real conversation can take place, which allows the adolescent to feel comfortable talking to his or her parents—something most teens don't feel they can do. This can become an important factor when a teenager is faced with social problems involving sex and drugs and needs an adult opinion. If they can't talk to their parents about the weather, then they certainly won't be able to talk to them about the more sensitive issues.

Some signs that the hormones are creating a need for independence are much more overt than having opinions and arguing. These physical differences between teenagers and parents, are mostly guaranteed to upset the elders, but are necessary to indicate clearly to parents that their children are now different from them. They include musical choice, clothing, hairstyles, piercing, and tattoos. In each generation there are fads in one or more of these areas that upset parents. Music has also been an integral part of the teenaged years, usually much to the displeasure of most of their parents. In the 1950s, 60s, and 70s it was the hairstyles that set teens apart from their parents. Starting with Elvis's oiled-back ducktail and proceeding through the Beatles and the acid-rock groups, teenage hairstyles became more and more outrageous. Recently, hairstyles have not been a major concern for parents, but piercing various parts of the body and having a cool "tat" certainly have. As it turns out, parental condemnation of these fads is an important part of the process. By becoming upset with the music a teenager is listening to, the clothing he or she is wearing, or the part of the body that has been pierced, parents are tacitly recognizing that the teen is different from them. That is exactly what the teens need. While they are not consciously aware of why they like the styles and music that they do, they feel more independent and grown-up when they make a decision in these areas that upsets their parents.

Parents must recognize their adolescent's need to be different from them and not take it personally. Adults often refer to the teenage need to be different as "rebellion" but it really isn't a revolt against parental standards, only a need to be different from them. If parents want their child to change what they are listening to or wearing, then expressing disapproval is not the way to do it. This only validates the teen's identity and will create major battles in the family. It is far more effective to ignore the fad when it is not life-threatening or not against your moral code. It will pass. Reading through your own high-school yearbooks will give considerable insight into the universality of teenage fads and help to reduce your outrage. Teenagers need to feel different, and most of their ways of doing so are harmless.

If the methods chosen by a teenager to express independence clearly contravene a family moral code, then it is well within parental rights to modify the behaviour. This can rarely be done by simply banning the practice. If, for example, a teenage daughter wants to wear clothing that is too immodest for parental standards, then banning that clothing will keep her from wearing it at home, but the teen will find ways to get around this ban at school or at the mall. She will simply keep another set of clothing in her school locker or at a friend's. It is far more effective to initiate a discussion with the teen to find out why she wants to wear such clothes and to find a compromise that is acceptable to all. While parents may not think they have to compromise, it usually works better to do so. If an edict must be passed, parents need to realize that it will have to be enforced. This can become tedious and contentious, but it can be done—with effort. In most cases, however, a compromise can be found and both parents and teens are happy.

Finally, hormones not only create a need to be different in teenagers, they also initiate mood swings. For several years the hormone flow into the system is not regular, but seems to come in spurts. Hormones are very powerful chemicals and can turn a happy, outgoing teen into an irritable grump. A parallel to this phenomenon is menopause in women. This is the reverse of puberty in that the hormones that allow pregnancy are disappearing, resulting in mood swings that make great material for comics but are very difficult when actually being experienced. Teen moods need to be recognized by parents as a natural part of the adolescent process and they should not be taken personally. Once again, the teen can't control these feelings, so there is no need to get angry with a moody, irritable adolescent. Instead, when snapped at for a perfectly reasonable request, a parent might say, "Wow. You really seem down today," rather than, "You don't have to be so snotty about it." The former statement recognizes the mood while the latter is guaranteed to result in an argument. This does not mean that parents have to put up with rudeness or temper tantrums. It just means that they should deal with the situation with calmness and understanding, while insisting that their request be honoured.

Brain Redevelopment

While hormones have long been known to create teenage behaviour changes, many puzzling behaviours could not be explained by hormones alone. In recent years, some of the gaps in understanding teens have been filled in by brain research. Studies utilizing functional magnetic resonance imaging (fMRI), which measures blood flow in the brain and spinal cord, show that during the teen years the brain is undergoing changes. While many areas of the research are still controversial, there is little doubt that brain changes are taking place, and that these changes can account for some of the puzzling behaviours of the teen years. What seems to be happening is that, in order to become more efficient, the brain is pruning the number of connections between the neurons and further insulating the neurons that are frequently used. While this process is occurring, some functions of the teenage brain do not work as well as those of adult brains, particularly in the area of decision making. Researchers have shown that teens need to use much more of their brain—particularly the prefrontal cortex—to make decisions than adults do. This is because, due to the youngsters' lack of experiences in life, other areas of the brain have not yet taken over part of this management process. Adults are therefore able to make faster and better decisions than teens.

- **Impulsive Behaviour**
  What this means is that teenagers often do dumb things because their brain has not yet fully developed. Often the teens themselves will say,

"I made a bad choice." This is correct and yet not quite accurate. Teens often make these poor choices because of the immaturity of their brains and not because of selfishness or maliciousness. Further research indicates that when teens make choices or decisions, they actually think more about them than adults do—then often make the wrong choice anyway. Apparently teenage brains can weigh the pros and cons of a particular decision before choosing the wrong path. Their lack of experience in life combined with their brain's tendency to give the positive aspects of the decision greater weight than the potential negative consequences often allows them to choose the more interesting, exciting, or rewarding path, rather then the morally correct one. An example of the teenage decision-making process might be useful.

An adolescent enters a convenience store intending to purchase a chocolate bar and a soft drink. He notices that the clerk is busy with another customer and that no one is looking his way. He thinks, "I could just take that chocolate bar and no one would know the difference." Then he might think, "Yeah, but that would be stealing. If I got caught, I'd be in trouble." If his brain stopped at this point all would be well. But unfortunately it doesn't. Instead he reasons, "But no one is looking and I could get the bar for free." That does it; the decision is made. Quickly, he stuffs the bar into his pocket and starts out the door, only to be stopped by the clerk, who saw him swipe the bar in the security mirror.

The parents are then called and angrily storm into the store, demanding to know how the boy could have done such a dumb thing, especially since he had the money for the bar in his pocket. Didn't he know that stealing was wrong? Hadn't they taught him better than that? The teen has no answer for these questions because he himself can't figure out why he had "decided" to steal the chocolate bar.

Impulsive behaviour is one of the hallmarks of teenagers, perhaps the one that most drives parents crazy. Whether it is "borrowing" the family car without permission, spraying graffiti on a wall, smashing the windows of a vacant house, or chugging an entire bottle of alcohol, these impulsive acts are behind the fearsome reputation the teenage years hold in parents' minds. Since the great majority of these acts are the products of a redeveloping brain, there is no need for parents to get angry with their children for engaging in them. This is a key point for parents and stepparents of teenagers. They are not doing these things on purpose or to upset their parents. They are not doing them out of selfishness or spite. However, this does not mean that these impulsive acts should simply be forgiven and forgotten. If the teenager has done something that is against the parents' moral code or the family rules, then consequences are definitely in order. The only difference is that when parents realize the true origins of the behaviour, anger and lectures are not necessary. For teens to learn to make fewer and fewer impulsive "decisions" as they get older, there must be consequences to remind them not to do these things and to further develop the brain. As the teen gains experience and the other areas of the brain begin to help out with the decision-making process, then such actions should cease.

- **Risk-Taking**

Another characteristic of teenage behaviour that is driven by this brain reorganization is the tendency to take risks. Adults often think of this tendency as the fearlessness of youth or as a need to experiment, but it seems actually to be a salient feature of the teenage brain. In boys, this trend is easy to see as they ride their bikes off minor cliffs and over large obstacles, or snowboard over huge jumps or down rails. Girls tend to be subtler in their risk-taking behaviour but it is definitely there. They will take risks with sex or in trying drugs, rather than in more obvious ways. Since boys will do these things, too, girls are not usually considered risk-takers, but parents need to realize that female adolescents definitely take risks in areas where, once again, parents expect them to "know better." Whenever parents realize that their teens are indulging in risky behaviours, they need to utilize this understanding in dealing with the actions. While consequences are not always necessary, discussing the situation calmly can help to prevent recurrence of the undesirable behaviour.

Suppose, for example, that a young teenager of either sex comes home drunk from a party. Anger will serve no purpose in dealing with an inebriated teen. Instead, the parents need to send the teen to bed and deal with the situation in the morning. The next day they should start the conversation with, "What happened?" rather than, "How could you be so stupid?" After hearing their child's story, it may be necessary to impose consequences, or perhaps the hangover will be punishment enough. In either case, parents must realize that teens tend to engage in risk-taking behaviour due to some need from within their brain rather than because they rationally decided to do these dangerous things. That knowledge will help the parents to stay calm and deal more effectively with the situation, rather than thinking that there is a problem with their parenting or that they have a bad kid.

Jenna, a 16-year-old grade 10 student, had never been much of a drinker. In fact, she had hardly touched alcohol at previous parties and gatherings. Knowing this, her parents were stunned one Saturday night to receive a call from the local hospital. Jenna was in serious condition with a severe case of alcohol poisoning. Talking with her concerned friends elicited the facts of the incident. Jenna and her friends had been discussing the pros and cons of drinking alcohol at the party and had decided that it wasn't so bad if they were careful. Jenna took a drink of straight vodka and, while she didn't really like the taste, decided that it wasn't having any effect on her. She then filled her water glass to the brim with the booze and drank it straight down. Again she felt no immediate effects so she did it again. In total, she probably drank about 15 ounces of straight alcohol in just a few minutes. Within an hour she had passed out and, being unable to revive her, her friends took Jenna to the hospital.

In discussing the situation the next day, it turned out that Jenna knew very little about the effects of alcohol on the body. She expected that she would feel them immediately, so when nothing happened right away, she reasoned that the alcohol was not affecting her and that she could safely drink more. She had wanted to try drinking to see what it was like but, like most teens, she did not have the knowledge and experience to know how to do it safely.

This incident did not require consequences. Jenna's brush with death resulted in a very sick girl for several days thereafter. This incident pointed out a gap in the teen's knowledge that had never been addressed, either by her parents or by school programs. Parents need to talk about sex, alcohol, other drugs, and all other possible risk behaviours with their teens before they "experiment" with them. Unfortunately, this is rarely done, and all too often teens are left to discover the facts for themselves.

- **Chores**

One of the key problem areas between parents of all kinds is the tendency of teenagers not to do their assigned tasks. Chores are one of the main battlegrounds between teens and all types of parents. Those who marry parents of teenagers and are thus presented with a ready-made family of one or more adolescents are particularly frustrated by this teen tendency. Once again, the main culprit appears to be in the teenage brain. Teens appear to have difficulties with sequencing tasks. Any chore, from room cleaning to dishwashing, involves a sequence of steps. In dishwashing, for example, teenagers have to:

- collect the dishes
- put them in the dishwasher

- add detergent
- close the door, and
- turn the machine on.

Teens appear to get confused in the process of sorting all these steps out and, during these short periods of confusion, often get distracted by something more important—such as calling a friend about the weekend. In fact, this distraction can occur even as the teen is walking toward the kitchen. Their brains seem to get easily confused and distracted so that, even when they intend to do the chores, they often fail to do so.

When I surveyed a large number of teens for my first book, they were unanimous in declaring that they should have chores. That fact alone was an eye-opener for many parents, since their children were all so terrible at actually completing them. Parents think that the teens are just lazy and don't want to do their chores. Given the boring and repetitive nature of the tasks, there may be an element of truth to the not-wanting-to-do-them part, but the real reason behind their failure to complete assigned tasks is actually found in their distractibility and poor sequencing capabilities. This knowledge can help parents to stay calm and deal with the situation more effectively.

Dealing with the situation means getting the teens actually to complete their assigned jobs. Parents need to utilize the PPH approach—Patience, Persistence, and Humour. The fact is that teens should have chores to do, as they help to build responsibility and self-discipline. It's just that parents cannot expect that teenagers will see the need to do a job and then complete it. In reality, they don't usually notice that their clothes are lying all over the living room or that they have left their dishes on the coffee table. They also forget their weekly assignments such as room cleaning or taking the garbage out. As a result, parents must actually be a part of the chore-finishing process, *but not by doing them*. Many parents get so frustrated with trying to get their teens to do their chores that they end up doing the jobs themselves.

This is counter-productive as it teaches the kids nothing about responsibility. It is definitely hard work to get the teens to develop this sense of responsibility, but it is well worth it in the end.

The first step is Patience. The process of teaching teens to be self-starters and finishers of routine tasks is going to take years. While adults can learn new tasks in days or weeks, teens, because of their redeveloping brains, will require years. This may be frustrating, but it is the simple truth of the matter, and the sooner parents realize this, the less frantic frustration they will experience. This in turn will reduce the number of arguments with the teenager. Patience is required to repeat the same reminders over and over; the rewards are well worth the wait.

Next comes Persistence. This means that not only can you not give up on the teens, you have to make a special effort to keep on top of them so that they get the assigned tasks completed. To do this, parents need to be a combination of foreman and cheerleader. In other words, they need to ensure that jobs get done, just as a foreman would on a job site, but in a supportive and enthusiastic way. Parental reminders are often given in a nagging way, which irritates the teenager and results in an argument. Instead, these prompts need to be given positively. A cheerleader would be yelling, "Go Team Go" in an effort to get the best from their team; a parent needs to be using a similar approach, such as, "Come on Jason, you can do it. Let's get it done." Parents have to keep after their teens until the jobs get done, but must do so in as supportive a way as possible. It is certainly more work than doing the job themselves, but teaches the teen that they need to take some responsibility around the house as well.

The final ingredient is Humour. The use of small jokes, or at least a relaxed attitude while trying to get teens to do their chores, helps to keep conflict out of the situation. Getting upset with the teen will almost always result in an argument. The teens know they should be doing their chores, but they don't really know why they have difficulty getting them done. They have no idea that the answer lies partially in brain redevelopment. This tends to make them defensive and touchy. A calm, humorous reminder is far more effective than a nagging, whiny one in preventing the teen's defensive mechanisms from kicking in. If the parent stays calm, the situation will not escalate. Humour helps to show that the parent is not upset. It may be hard for some parents to be humorous when the kitchen is a mess, but it can be done. Statements such as, "Oh my gosh! Who bombed our kitchen?" get the message across far more effectively than, "This kitchen's a mess. Can't you even remember to do a simple job?" If humour is not your style, then at least make the reminder a simple statement like, "Let's go, Trina, time to clean up the kitchen." Delivered lightly and calmly, this will work almost as well as a humorous turn of phrase.

The PPH approach takes into account the teenager's difficulties in sequencing tasks and remembering to do them, and helps to teach responsibility and self-discipline. It is vital that teenagers learn these skills and just as vital that parents teach them in the most effective possible way.

- **Sleep Patterns**
A majority of parents complain that their teens won't go to bed at night, and then can't get out of bed to go to school in the morning. The result is that every morning is a battle, with the parent wisely saying, "If you would go to bed earlier, you'd be able to get up in the morning." While this makes sense, actually doing it is far more difficult for the teens than it sounds because their brains are interfering with the process.

While researchers have no idea why it happens, our circadian rhythms change during the adolescent years. In the evening, young children and adults feel sleepy. A sleeping person's brain goes through cycles of deep sleep and relatively light sleep. In the light sleep, people dream, while in the deep sleep periods, the brain is undergoing repair and reconstruction work. Both types of sleep seem to be necessary for human survival. The problem with adolescent brains is that in the late evening they have a wake cycle when they feel wide awake. To make matters worse, they are usually in a deep sleep cycle at the time that they are supposed to wake up. This is the opposite of adults and young children. This means that they can't go to sleep easily when they should and they can't wake up quickly for school at the appointed time.

This different sleep cycle places teens in a difficult position. Parents tell them to go to sleep early—usually around 10 o'clock at night, but they can't. They are wide awake. Then their parents get mad at them for not springing happily out of bed in the morning when, once again, they can't because their brains are befogged by sleep. The result is usually a morning battle with everyone leaving the house grumpy. To make matters worse, teens need an average of 9.25 hours of sleep each night to feel rested, but our society conspires to make this very difficult. Television, video games, and brain redevelopment help to keep the kids up late, while school busing and parental work schedules make it mandatory for them to get up very early in the morning. This means that teens are usually sleep deprived during the week, which not only makes them more irritable, but also drives them to sleep in until noon on weekends. This latter tendency causes many parents to consider them to be lazy; when, really, all that is happening is that their young bodies are catching up. If you consider that most teenagers will not get to sleep until about 11:00 PM, then must rise between 6:30 and 7:00 AM, it is obvious that they will get only about eight hours of sleep each night. This puts them in a 6.25-hour sleep deficit by the end of the week, so they make it up on the weekends. There is no need to consider them to be indolent and be angry with them. The teens have no idea what is going on. They just know they are tired, so they sleep in. What could be more logical?

Parents need to understand the biological basis of teenage sleep behaviour so that they don't get angry at it. The teens themselves have no idea what is going on, but even if they did, they couldn't change it. What parents can do is to ensure that their teenagers are at least in bed by 10:00 PM, even if they can't sleep yet. They can be allowed to read if they wish, but they have to be in the sack. Parents should also ensure that their kids are not doing anything exciting in the hour or so prior to bedtime, such as playing video games or being on computer chat lines. In the morning, parents need to use that PPH approach again. Parents must realize that getting up will not be easy for the teen, so they need to assist in the process. This means actually going into the room to wake them up, then checking back to see that they are up. It might take three calls and, if no results have been obtained by the third, they may have to stay in the room, telling stories about when they were teens. If this doesn't get the teen up—nothing will.

Since everybody is a bit different as to exactly how much sleep they need, there will be many different reactions in the morning. However, most adolescents will be difficult to waken and parents need to be prepared for this. In a humorous spirit, one parent played marches on the family stereo every morning. It started as a joke, but it worked so well he kept it up. Understanding the nature of teen sleeping patterns and the need for the PPH approach will allow families to start each day off on a much more pleasant note.

The combination of the onset of the hormones necessary to redevelop the adolescent brain is now known to cause the behaviours that so often frustrate and upset parents. These behaviours have previously been lumped into such categories as rebelliousness or experimentation, and have generally been considered by parents to be fully within a teenager's control. They are not. The teen years are a time of development and maturation. If parents understand these processes, they can deal with the behaviours effectively. This might entail ignoring them, using the PPH approach, or even assessing penalties. Whatever has to be done when a teenager exhibits negative behaviours can be accomplished more effectively when the parents are calm than when anger enters the picture. As has been said so often throughout this book, nothing good ever results from anger. Understanding the origins of teen behaviour allows parents to maintain control; they can understand it and can deal with it. When this approach is taken, parents can actually enjoy the teen years. In fact, these can be the best parenting years of all. The children are now old enough to have conversations with and to do things with—skiing, biking, shopping—on a relatively equal basis. They can be fun years for parents and teenagers as long as the parents understand the true nature of their teenagers.

Stepparents and Teenagers

As has been mentioned, the challenge for stepparents confronted with frustrating teenage behaviours is the lack of a biological bond. When you have raised the kids from birth, your deep love for them allows you to tolerate more than you can when they are not your children. The tendency for many stepparents is to think that these adolescents have been very badly raised, and they blame their new partner and his or her ex-spouse for not doing a better job. While this may occasionally be true, much more often the problem will be that the stepparent simply does not understand the origins of the frustrating behaviours and, rather than dealing with them calmly and effectively, takes them as a personal attack and overreacts. The key for stepparents is to understand the basis of their newly acquired teenager's behaviour and to use this understanding to stay calm and patient when dealing with some of the more frustrating aspects of their conduct.

The problems that teenage behaviour cause for all parents usually fall into two main areas—communication and discipline. However, for stepparents there is a third problem area—the behaviours created in the teenager by emotions resulting from the parents' divorce—their breakup baggage. Each of these areas needs to be understood as thoroughly as possible if the stepparent is to develop a relationship with the teenagers and actually enjoy living with them.

Breakup Baggage

While this subject was addressed in detail in the first chapter, the effect of these very powerful emotions on teenagers cannot be underestimated. When the effects of hormones and brain reorganization meet the emotions caused by divorce, the already puzzling behaviours of teenagers become magnified. Behaviours that might just have been annoying become almost impossible for unsuspecting stepparents to deal with when this baggage is added to the mix. A case history will illuminate this point more clearly.

Cayley was a pleasant 16-year-old when her father suddenly decided to remarry. He and his ex-wife had had a messy divorce with considerable acrimony for many years. Cayley's mom had remarried and her husband had taken up her cause with a vengeance. Although the divorce had taken place 10 years ago, issues were constantly surfacing, mostly associated with money. At one point, the younger daughter, 14 at the time, had expressed a desire to come and live with her dad. Her mother had then threatened to sell her horse if she did. Since horses were a major focus in the young teen's life, she reluctantly stayed with her mother and stepfather on the acreage.

Because of the turbulence of the divorce and its considerable breakup baggage, the father decided not to remarry until his girls were grown and on their own. While he dated frequently, he purposely avoided commitment, much to the frustration of several hopeful girlfriends. However, his well-thought-out plans were shattered when he met Helen, a vivacious divorcée several years younger than him. After a whirlwind courtship of just a few months, Helen moved in with him and they announced plans to get married. At this point Cayley became angry. Up until then, she had been the more relaxed of the two girls, rarely arguing or giving her father any problems on her visitations. Suddenly she announced that it was her or Helen. If her dad remarried, she would have nothing further to do with him. How much of this anger was fuelled by the ex-wife is difficult to determine, but there is no doubt that she played a part. Still, the main problem was that Cayley was not prepared for her father to remarry, leaving her to play second fiddle to this unknown woman.

Unfortunately, the father did not take his daughter's anger seriously. In fact, he got angry in return, telling her that she had no right to interfere with his happiness. As a result, Cayley followed through on her threat and stopped speaking to her dad. Worse, she dropped out of school, became a member of a very wild crowd and, within a year, had a child by a rebellious, drug-addicted dropout. Attempts at reconciliation, especially in light of the new grandchild, proved fruitless, and the penniless couple moved far away from Cayley's father and his new bride.

While this may be an extreme case, it illustrates the power of breakup baggage. The poor stepmother, Helen, ended up feeling guilty that she had caused the rift between her new husband and his older daughter. She never even had the chance to get to know the girl. The major mistake here was that the father, spurred by his very strong feelings for Helen, had moved far too quickly for his daughter to accept. There needed to be a much longer "break-in" period for her to get to know Helen. The fact that the ex-wife was more than likely egging her daughter on by saying negative things about the prospective stepmother certainly did not help; however, this was not the main cause of the dispute. Cayley had had enough difficulty accepting her stepfather and did not want to go through those emotions again. At least then she had been younger and less independent in thought. She did not want to share her father and was not given enough time to get over these very strong feelings. Having her father meet them with anger only fuelled her frustration further and led to many more angry scenes before she finally moved away in protest.

In less severe cases, stepparents will often be faced with anger levels far above those to be expected from an actual situation. Suppose the stepfather mentions to his teenaged stepdaughter that she has forgotten to do her chores. This seems innocuous enough, but the response could be a violent outburst of anger and hostility that baffles and hurts the stepparent. What often results is an angry or defensive response from the stepparent that leads to many hurtful things being said by both parties. It is not the chores that are the problem—most teens get angry when reminded of chores they failed to do, but when there is frustration from the fact that dad or mom has remarried, then the anger is often out of proportion to the actual incident.

These intensely angry responses are common to teenagers, since they are rarely able to speak their minds. They form part of the independence of thought that they are developing in response to their hormones. While preparing the body to have children, these hormones are also preparing the child to move out and start a family of his or her own, independent of their parents and the decision-making help they have offered previously. They frequently make decisions that are poorly thought out because they do not have the emotional maturity required to make really serious choices, but they make them anyway. This causes them to decide that their parents should not have remarried and to act accordingly by taking out their anger about their biological parent's actions on the stepparent.

Not surprisingly, this can greatly annoy the unsuspecting stepparent coming into the family with the best of intentions. A constant barricade of anger and sarcasm can wear out these intentions pretty quickly. The stepparent then demands that the biological parent do something about the rude and rebellious child. Now the biological parent is caught in the middle between the new love and the children—a position almost impossible to resolve.

The solution is for the stepparent to understand the nature of teenagers and the power of breakup baggage. It is up to the adult to adjust to the child—not vice versa. Teenagers, while feigning knowledge and maturity far above their years, do not actually have the emotional maturity to overcome their feelings. Even when they realize that their parent is happy in the new marriage, they are unable to use this knowledge to overcome their very strong feelings. This should not be the case for the stepparents. They do have the maturity necessary to deal with this situation. Unfortunately, they often get caught up in the emotions because they do not expect to be met with resistance, thinking that because the parent loves them, their kids will, too. Before they realize what has happened, they are into the battle.

The secret for the stepparent lies in understanding the situation and preparing properly for it. If the steps for the dating process outlined in Chapter 2 are followed and the necessary time and effort is expended in getting to know the teenagers, then much of the anger will have dissipated well before the marriage takes place. If these steps have not been taken and the marriage has occurred rapidly, then the stepparent will need to have considerable patience and understanding to work through the teenager's breakup baggage and resistance to their presence. We're not just talking about a little patience here, but the patience of Job himself. It will take years before the situation stabilizes with teenagers, as their feelings can be much stronger than those of younger children.

Along with this patience, there must also be a constant effort to attend the teen's events and to interact with them. However, if the marriage has occurred quickly and has been "sprung on" the teen, then this effort needs to be delayed for several months, during which the youngster can get used to the stepparent's presence. Immediately thrusting the new spouse into the teen's life can have very negative effects and can backlash on the adults. After a period of several months, the stepparent can gradually start to attend events and even take the adolescent child on joint activities, such as shopping, to ball games, or just out for coffee.

The difficulty for the stepparent will be to deal with negative behaviours, such as rudeness, arguments, sarcasm, criticism, and even silence. This latter ploy may seem a welcome relief at first, but it can become a very annoying passive-aggressive tactic. All these devices must be met with calmness and understanding. While this can be difficult, practice will eventually allow the stepparent to become extremely effective in dealing with these behaviours. As an illustration, let's look at a typical tactic and its countermeasure.

SCOTT WOODING

Stepparent:	*"Can you please take your dishes into the kitchen and put them in the dishwasher?"*
Teen:	*"Why are you always on my case?"*
SP:	*"I don't think I am. I just want the house to be clean and tidy."*
Teen:	*"You're always bugging me about stuff. Why can't you just leave me alone?"*
SP:	*"I'm not trying to criticize. I'm only reminding you to keep the house as tidy as possible."*
Teen:	*"No you're not. You just like to bug me. I don't know why my dad married you. You're a real pain."*

This is a point where the conversation can deteriorate rapidly if the stepparent is not careful. Instead of saying something equally hurtful, it is better to say:

SP:	*"I'm sorry you feel that way. I'd rather not be on your case at all, but it is important to keep the house clean."*
Teen:	*"I hate you. I wish you'd never come into this house."*

Again, this is very hard to take, but keeping cool will be far more effective than saying "Well, I don't like you very much, either."

SP:	*"I know it can be hard for you sometimes. It takes time for everyone to adjust to a new situation. Please just put your dishes in the kitchen."*
Teen:	*"You're such a nag."*

Wow! That's harsh.

SP: *"I know it seems like that, but I don't mean to be. If you can try to keep the place tidy, I won't need to say anything."*

Teen: *"All you care about is this stupid house."*

SP: *"That's not true. I think you're a great person. Like most teens, you forget things sometimes."*

Teen: *"Fine! I'll take your stupid dishes."*

SP: *"Thanks very much. I appreciate it."*

It's easy to see how quickly such conversations can deteriorate. Trying to hurt back will never solve the problem. It will only enrage the teen and cause the gap between stepparent and child to widen further. If the stepparent doesn't stay cool, only negative things can result. While staying calm is a key to the process of dealing with breakup baggage and the initial resistance to a stepparent, this calmness must not be interpreted as passivity. It is often going to be necessary to take some action along with keeping your cool. Note that in the conversation above, the stepparent achieved the goal of getting the dishes picked up. This is an important point to remember. Staying calm does not mean standing there and taking abuse. It just means dealing with the situation calmly so that the situation will not get worse than it already is. Even if consequences are called for, they must be administered without anger if they are to be effective.

Teenagers can be very difficult to raise, even for natural parents, if their behaviour is not understood. When breakup baggage is added to difficult behaviour and the lack of a biological bond, the task becomes exponentially more complex. Stepparents need to be aware of the challenges that they will face in helping to raise someone else's teenagers. However, with practice, raising teens can actually be enjoyable and rewarding.

SCOTT WOODING

Communication

One of the least understood aspects of life with teenager behaviour is that they are poor communicators. As little children, most kids will talk freely and easily. In fact, it is often difficult to keep them quiet. Not so for teenagers. For reasons that are still not well understood, when children enter adolescence their communication skills atrophy. They just don't say much spontaneously. This baffles and frustrates adults because it gives them the impression that adolescents don't want to talk. This is not true; they are just not good communicators. This leaves it up to the adults in their lives to communicate with them.

If this is puzzling for biological parents, it is even more so for step-parents, who are very apt to take the lack of communication as an unwillingness to talk to them because they are not the teen's real parents. In other words, a teenager's lack of communication is often taken personally by stepparents and interpreted as "the silent treatment" rather than just part of normal teen behaviour. While this passive-aggressive tactic can be used by resentful teens, more often than not it is simply their natural tendency rather than a calculated behaviour.

Understanding that teens are poor communicators is vital because it means that the onus is on the adults to get them to talk rather than expecting that this will occur spontaneously. This communication is extremely important for parents and stepparents to have, as it is the only way to find out what is happening in the adolescents' lives. It is also the only way to be in a position to give advice when it is needed, such as in the key areas of sex and drugs. The good news is that teenagers really do want to talk to their parents; it's just that they are not very good at starting conversations. Fortunately there are some techniques that work well for stimulating these conversations, eliciting information about their lives, and giving the necessary advice.

Spending Relaxed Time

The key component to communicating with teenagers is very simple—you have to be there. In order for conversations to take place, parents and stepparents have to be in a relaxed setting with the teens. "Relaxed" is the key. No one communicates well when in a hurry or when intensely involved in something. Adults need to take the time to engage in relaxing activities with teenagers if they expect them to open up and talk. These need not be complex or expensive activities, just going shopping, walking the dog, hitting balls at the driving range, or going out for a coffee together will be enough to get conversations started. This seems simple enough, but it is not as easy as it sounds. Teenagers often have their own agendas that may not mesh with those of their parents. It may take two or three invitations before the teens will actually be available for these activities. Do not despair. That's completely normal. They may have made plans with friends, everyone may be on MSN at that time, or the teens may simply not be in the mood. Don't be discouraged by a few refusals; just keep asking them to do things and eventually they will acquiesce.

Another barrier can be the lack of time that parents and stepparents of this generation have to spend with their children. Work schedules have come to predominate over family time and it may take a conscious effort on the part of parents to take time to spend with the kids. All too often a hectic week at work is followed by a frantic weekend trying to catch up on the household chores. Precious time that could be spent with the kids just slips away. For a quick refresher course on how this happens and what the results are, just listen to Harry Chapin's brilliant song, "The Cat's in the Cradle."

Questioning

Just spending some relaxed time with teenagers does not guarantee that they will talk; it just sets the scene so that communication can happen. Often parents have to ask a few questions before the conversation will take on a life of its own. On average it seems to take about three questions before a discussion will develop. The trick is to be able to ask the right questions.

Questions that help open a conversation should revolve around the teenager's activities. These include school, extracurricular interests, as well as happenings with his or her friends. Some sample questions might be:

- How was basketball practice today?
- How do you think you did on the math test today?
- Are you still angry with Katie?
- How did Billy do at the track meet?
- How's that English assignment going?

It is important that parents not be discouraged by an initial monosyllabic response. It takes more than one question to get a conversation going with teenagers, so follow-ups to the above questions might be:

- When do you play your next game?
- Were the questions on the test what you expected?
- How did you patch things up?
- What events did he take part in?
- Do you have enough information on the subject?

A third round might even be necessary, but if parents are persistent, a conversation will eventually result. Note that in order to ask the right questions, parents need to know what their children's interests and activities are. This might sound simplistic, but it is amazing how few parents actually have this basic information. For example, in order to ask about a basketball practice or a math test, parents need to know that their teen has had one that day. It is a cyclical process. In order to gain information you have to have some information, which will give you more information to gather still more data.

Effective questioning is a crucial technique in communicating with a teenager. Parents should not be discouraged if occasionally it fails to elic-it much response. There will be days when teens just don't feel like talk-ing. They are, after all, subject to mood swings. However, usually this technique will work well when employed in a relaxed setting, and you will reap huge rewards.

Listening

There is no communication method that will work for long if the commu-nicator does not actively listen to the person he or she is talking to. Teens can tell very quickly if their parent is really interested in what they are say-ing by the body language being exhibited. If, for example, the parent con-tinues reading the paper, watching TV, or peeling the potatoes while con-versing, then the teen very quickly senses that their parent is just going through the motions. To listen effectively, parents must make eye contact and actively listen to the teens until they have completed what they were saying. Interrupting, correcting, or denying their feelings will all indicate that the parents are not really interested in what is being said, and com-munication will cease. The number one complaint that teenagers have about their parents is that they never listen to them. This will surprise most parents, as they actually think that they do listen. The truth is that they often don't, or they mean to but upset the teen by interrupting. Good lis-tening is the real key to effective communication with anyone, but it is par-ticularly important when conversing with impatient teenagers.

Discipline

The earlier chapter on discipline outlined the basic principles that steppar-ents need to follow in raising their stepchildren. However, as the title of this chapter indicates, teenagers are a special case. Because they are in a transitional stage between child and adult, they need a slightly different approach from that taken with younger children. The interesting fact is that teenagers want discipline. They actually prefer the structure imposed by setting rules and levying consequences for breaking them. This can be clearly seen in the school classroom. Teenagers would much rather have teachers who keep order than those who cannot control the class. However, there is one main difference between younger children and teenagers when it comes to discipline—teenagers want it to be "fair." It is the interpretation of this word that creates much of the difficulty for parents in determining the most effective disciplinary approach for their families.

Because teenagers are older and their reasoning power is more developed than that of younger children, they have a need to understand the reasons behind the rules and guidelines imposed on them. If they don't, they consider these rules to be unfair. The key for all parents is to involve their teens in the rule-setting process. When they have input into the setting of the rules, teens feel that the process is fair. In fact, it is. Many parents might consider this to be akin to allowing the inmates to run the asylum, but they will be surprised at how effective it can be. When they are given some responsibility, teens are much more sensible and reasonable than adults realize.

The technique for obtaining teenage input into the household rules is to have yearly meetings on this subject. The best time for these meetings is in late August, just before the new school year begins. The meeting should include all the teens in the family and should begin with the parents asking what rules need to be added, changed, or modified. This process not only allows for input from the adolescents, but also gives a formal structure to the rule-setting process. Most parents set their rules on the fly—when a problem occurs, they make a rule. If the teen comes in from a party later than expected, a curfew is set. This outrages the teenager, largely because they had no input into this new guideline. A meeting where the teens are allowed to make suggestions is far more effective. The bonus is that the adolescents engaged in the process have no comeback when they break a rule and receive consequences. After all, they helped to set the rule.

Parents will also be stunned at how sensible the teens will be in this process. When they know that their suggestions will be seriously considered, teenagers can to be very responsible and mature. If they do get frivolous, then parents are not obligated to accept the suggestion; however, this will not happen if the atmosphere in the meeting clearly indicates that the parents are willing to listen and to consider the suggestions. Compromise can also be an important part of this process. If the parents and teens are too far apart in their ideas, then meeting in the middle can leave both sides happy. Take the curfew, for example. All teens should have one as protection for themselves as well as peace of mind for the parents. If the teen suggests 2:00 AM and the adults want 12:00 AM, then perhaps 1:00 AM can be the compromise. The idea is for everyone to win, and for neither the parents nor the teens to be dictators.

For stepparents, following this process can be particularly effective. This is especially true when the stepparent tends to be the stricter parent. If teenagers feel that this new person in their lives is controlling their natural parent in the rule-setting procedure, then resentment will follow. The stepparent will then see the many ways that teens have to display their displeasure and resistance. A meeting with both parents present, and one where the teen's ideas are listened to and adopted where feasible, will go a long way toward diffusing any resentment the youngster might have about the stepparent. If the meeting is conducted democratically, with everyone getting a chance to speak, then both parents can clearly be seen to be on the same wavelength in this regulating process, rather than one or the other having to be the disciplinarian. What must be avoided is to have only one parent do all the negotiating—especially if that one parent is of the "step" variety.

Recognizing that teenagers are different from younger children, and allowing them some input into the family rules and regulations, will make the process "fair"; however, do not expect adolescents to thank their parents when consequences have to be imposed for a rule infraction. The teens will still grumble and complain at the time, but, because they recognize the ultimate fairness of this system, they will not harbour long-term grudges and resentment that will translate into a battle between teens and their stepparents.

SCOTT WOODING

Consequences

Modern parents are so concerned that punitive discipline will forever damage their teenager's fragile psyche that they often are not sure if they should give consequences at all. They definitely should. Remember, the purpose of discipline is to teach moral behaviour. The only way to do this effectively is to hand out consequences when family values are breached. The trick is to use the right ones.

For teens, the most effective consequence is the removal of a privilege. This may include banning video games for a day or two, taking away computer privileges, or confiscating the cell phone for a few days. These consequences are highly effective as such electronics are an integral part of the modern teen's life. They hate not having access to these things.

Grounding, as discussed in Chapter 5, should be reserved for only the most serious rule infractions, including drunkenness and the use of drugs. It just doesn't work very well—especially if it goes on too long. Parents and stepparents should not be concerned about getting the consequence just right. It doesn't matter what the consequence is as long as it is imposed immediately and doesn't last too long. Otherwise resentment builds and arguments result.

Combining an understanding of the nature of teenage behaviour with effective communication and disciplinary techniques can help to bridge the biological gap between teenagers and stepparents. While it is most successful if this knowledge is gained before inheriting teenagers, it is never too late to try to develop a relationship with them. It is certainly well worth the effort, both for the stepparent-stepchild relationship and for the sake of a future with the parent of those teens.

Chapter 8

Grandparents

In the flurry of activities and emotions that surround divorces and remarriages involving children, there is a forgotten group of people. These are the parents of those adults involved. They are the grandparents and potential stepgrandparents of the children of divorce. Rarely are their thoughts or feelings considered in any of the events that surround the breakup and reconstitution of the marriages of their own progeny. This is both understandable and unfortunate. It is understandable in that the children of these people are adults who are responsible for their own lives. They are no longer obligated to check with their parents before they do anything, even something as serious as divorce or remarriage.

Not taking the feelings and concerns of their parents into consideration when making these major decisions is also unfortunate, for a number of reasons. First, the biological grandparents have had to stand on the sidelines and watch their children go through the agony of divorce and worry about what effects the marital breakup might have on their grandchildren. Grandparenting is truly a joy for that great majority of parents who love their own brood. An almost mystical delight results from the presence of these youngsters in their lives. Most grandparents want to take an active part in the development of these young lives and enjoy their frequent presence. Suddenly their lives are thrown into turmoil by the divorce of their child, which can jeopardize not only their grandchildren's mental health but also their own ability even to see their grandchildren anymore. This can be a huge emotional shock for them.

Another unfortunate aspect of divorce and remarriage occurs for the parents of someone who is marrying a person with kids of his or her own. Just as suddenly as biological grandparents can lose contact with their grandkids, these people gain grandchildren, and are expected to treat these children as if they were their own grandchildren, even when there is no blood tie.

For many stepgrandparents this is no problem. Perhaps because they have no other grandkids, or simply because they love children, they can immediately assume the expected role. Others may not be as fortunate. They truly may have loved the ex-spouse and were upset to lose him or her

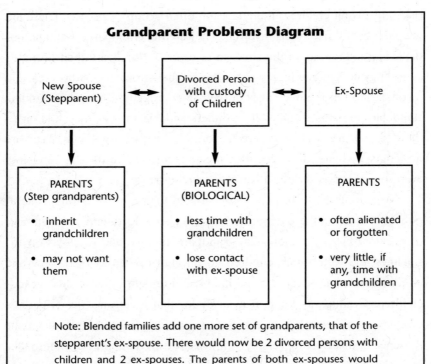

Grandparent Problems Diagram

New Spouse (Stepparent)	Divorced Person with custody of Children	Ex-Spouse

PARENTS (Step grandparents)	PARENTS (BIOLOGICAL)	PARENTS
• inherit grandchildren	• less time with grandchildren	• often alienated or forgotten
• may not want them	• lose contact with ex-spouse	• very little, if any, time with grandchildren

Note: Blended families add one more set of grandparents, that of the stepparent's ex-spouse. There would now be 2 divorced persons with children and 2 ex-spouses. The parents of both ex-spouses would experience similar problems.

SCOTT WOODING

as an in-law; they may not be comfortable with someone else's children; or they may not be comfortable with the age group of the children—as in the case of instant teenaged grandchildren. In these cases, they may have great difficulty adopting this new role.

The result of many of these situations can be extreme tension between these grandparents and potential stepgrandparents and their children. While this is not one of the most important issues surrounding stepparenting and blending families, it is one that needs at least some consideration and attention if problems with the parents of those directly involved are to be avoided.

Biological Grandparents

The unfortunate reality for biological grandparents in divorce situations is that they have no real power to affect the situation. It is up to the parents of the children to decide how much contact the grandparents of their ex-spouse will have with their grandchildren. Once the custodial parent has remarried and starts a new life, then there is little doubt that they will see much less of the youngsters if that parent is not their own child. They certainly can see them if their son or daughter has frequent visitation or if there is shared custody, but they will still be sharing the children with the new stepgrandparents, and their time will be more restricted than before the divorce.

The key for custodial parents is to try to keep any lingering breakup baggage from clouding their vision about their ex-spouses' parents. If these grandparents have not been actively involved in the divorce and have previously had a good relationship with their grandchildren, then it would be cruel to deny them access. The grandparents will normally be very apprehensive about what the situation with the grandkids will be, but most will be hesitant to say anything. It is up to the custodial parent to reassure them that they still have a part in the children's lives. This action takes a very mature person, especially if the breakup has been particularly rancorous. In fact, even if the divorce has been relatively amicable, it is still the breakup of a marriage, which is never pleasant. Negative feelings of any kind towards the ex-spouse often cause the custodial parents to restrict the grandparents' access to their children. Cutting the grandparents out of the children's lives is unfair both to them and to the grandchildren if the ex-spouse's parents have taken no part in the divorce proceedings.

The situation is much more complicated if the grandparents have been active participants in the divorce. Custodial parents will have a much harder time in allowing access to their children while the kids are in their care. In these cases, it would be reasonable to talk to the children about their desires. Even if the children are very young, they will have feelings about their grandparents. Divorce is hard enough on kids without cutting people they love out of their lives. If the kids have a strong desire to visit these grandparents, then the mature thing to do is to allow it, no matter how strong the parental feelings are about these people. The point to remember is that most of these grandparents were only supporting their child and probably were only hearing a very biased account of the marital problems. If, on the other hand, they were particularly vicious in their defence of their child, then it would be asking way too much of a parent to have anything more to do with them. What access their own child allows will be all they should be permitted. Hopefully, these cases are the minority.

One of the most difficult aspects of this biological grandparent situation is the new stepparents' feelings in this matter. Having a set of grandparents left over from the spouse's previous marriage, specifically the parents of the ex-spouse, can be difficult to accept and to deal with rationally. They are a constant reminder of the earlier relationship and many stepparents who are somewhat insecure in their new relationship may resent the grandparents' presence in their spouse's life. This must not be allowed to occur or it may become an "issue" in the new marriage. Stepparents need to understand that these people have a biological relationship with their newly acquired stepchildren that should not be interfered with. This relationship may have to be somewhat curtailed due to the presence of the stepgrandparents and the need to also spend time with them, but it would

SCOTT WOODING

be unwise to try to end this relationship completely. If the ex-spouse's parents wish to stay involved in their grandchildren's lives, then allowances need to be made for this. Certainly it is complex and confusing at times, but it is one of the realities of stepparenting and blending families.

Stepgrandparents

With grandparents who have blood ties to the grandkids, it is presumed that they will want to see these children frequently, but it is the custodial parent who plays the key role in how often these visits occur. In the cases of parents who inherit grandchildren through the marriage of their son or daughter, it is more up to these new grandparents as to how much they want to participate in the children's lives. Hopefully they will accept their stepgrandchildren with open arms. This is important in establishing the new family traditions that were discussed earlier. Christmas, Hanukkah, Easter, birthdays, and summer holidays are all important times for children, and grandparents can be a key part of these traditions. Christmas is a good example of the importance of involving grandparents, as this holiday is the granddaddy of all family times. How they react to Christmas is the very essence of a family. The traditions of the former family can soon be replaced by new ones if the stepgrandparents choose to participate.

If, in rare cases, the grandparents choose not to get actively involved, the biological parent must be very careful to try to understand the reasons behind this choice. Perhaps they already have a large number of biological grandchildren, or they may be intimidated by the age of the kids in the case of teenagers. No matter, this stepgrandparental choice can become a battle ground between the biological parent of the children and the new spouse if it is allowed to be. It is vital to remember that the grandparents played no part in their child's choices, but it does not mean that they are not happy with this choice. There may be very valid reasons that they do not want to be stepgrandparents. This must be viewed as their loss and accepted. Other traditions can be established instead.

While the couple who came in to the counsellor for a relationship problem had several contentious issues, the main one was the apparent "rejection" of the wife and her two young children by her new husband's parents. They rarely invited the couple to their home for supper and chose to spend the entire winter, including Christmas, in Arizona. Examination of the issue showed that, even as parents, this older couple had been distant. They had two other children, who also had kids of their own, but they, too, were rarely invited over. None were ever invited to spend time in Arizona. It seems that they simply did not really like kids that much, despite having had three of their own. This should not have become a marital issue, but the new wife, being defensive of her own children, was unable to see the reality of the situation. She could not accept her husband's explanation as she felt he was simply trying to make her feel better. The fact was that it was not her and her kids that were the problemThese stepgrandparents simply were not that involved in the parenting process and, having done their duty, had retreated into their own lives. It took a neutral party to explain this and, once it was understood, the issue went away.

While this may not be one of the biggest stepparenting issues, the consideration of grandparents' feelings and the understanding of their behaviour can not only be of benefit to the children, but can also contribute to greater harmony in the marriage. If grandparents are not behaving as they may be expected to, it is important that this behaviour not be taken personally. It is, in fact, unlikely to be personally directed but just a function of the type of people the grandparents are. It is far more important in these cases to focus on the marriage itself, rather than the distracting influence of someone's parents.

SCOTT WOODING

Epilogue

This book had two main purposes. The first was to warn prospective stepparents of the difficulties involved in raising someone else's children. Somehow, in the glow of love for the children's mother or father, far too many people miss the fact that stepparenting without recognizing the hazards is a potential minefield for remarriages. This is never the children's fault. The divorce and the all-too-frequent breakup baggage that accompanies it will usually have had serious effects on their ability to trust other adults. A prospective stepparent's love for their parent is not enough by itself to overcome their fears and worries about the newcomer.

The second purpose was to demonstrate how the stepparenting process can actually be done successfully, despite the pitfalls. Children want stability in their lives and they definitely want adults who love them to be present throughout their formative years. It's just that for stepparenting to be successful, it must be done slowly and carefully. Both the prospective stepparent and the parent of the children must be aware of the potential problems and take early steps to counter them. When this happens, the family will almost always bond effectively and the children will be much happier than they were with their single-parenting situation.

INDEX

SCOTT WOODING